BARRON'S
BUSINESS KEYS

# KEYS TO READING AN ANNUAL REPORT

## Fourth Edition

**George Thomas Friedlob, Ph.D., C.P.A.**
**and**
**Ralph E. Welton, Ph.D.**

*School of Accountancy & Legal Studies*
*Clemson University*
*Clemson, South Carolina*

*All inquiries should be addressed to:*
Barron's Educational Series, Inc.
250 Wireless Boulevard
Hauppauge, NY 11788
**www.barronseduc.com**

*Library of Congress Catalog Card Number 2007049114*

ISBN-13: 978-0-7641-3915-4
ISBN-10: 0-7641-3915-0

**Library of Congress Cataloging-in-Publication Data**
Friedlob, G. Thomas.
   Keys to reading an annual report / George Thomas Friedlob and
Ralph E. Welton. — 4th ed.
      p.  cm. — (Barron's business keys)
   Includes bibliographical references and index.
   ISBN-13: 978-0-7641-3915-4
   ISBN-10: 0-7641-3915-0
      1. Financial statements.  2. Auditors' reports.  I. Welton, Ralph E.
II. Title.

   HF5681.B2F773    2008
   657'.3—dc22                                    2007049114

PRINTED IN CHINA

9 8 7 6 5 4 3 2 1

# CONTENTS

# 1
# UNDERSTANDING THIS BOOK

This book is organized in 60 short keys. Each offers an immediately practical explanation of some vital aspect of annual reporting. The text is designed to be read either straight through or in random order, selecting topics as questions arise. If you do not understand the significance of long-term debt, for instance, you can simply look it up. There is a key on long-term (noncurrent) debt, another key specifically devoted to bonds and amortization, and still another key on debt and equity that will assist you in evaluating the company's level of long-term borrowing. Consult the index as a cross-reference to determine what subjects are covered in all the keys.

The book concludes with a list of questions and answers—the very questions (we hope) that you might ask us if we were close friends or business associates. Reading through this section is a good way to obtain an overview of the book and the basics of understanding annual reports.

Understanding accounting and financial reporting is a formidable yet achievable learning objective. The Securities and Exchange Commission (SEC), the Financial Accounting Standards Board, and various committees of the American Institute of Certified Public Accountants have promulgated volumes of principles, standards, and rules to organize and regiment the financial reporting of businesses in the United States. To help you through this maze, the following keys are arranged to proceed through three levels:

1. Understanding the annual report components;
2. Understanding the financial statements contained in an annual report; and
3. Analyzing the financial statements using ratio analysis.

Excerpts from actual annual reports are used to illustrate points made in the text. In addition, it's a good idea to have an annual report at your side as you go through the keys. Read about current assets, then examine the current assets section of your financial report. Study depreciation methods, then look to see which methods your company uses.

This book is intended to be a working reference. Read it and prosper.

# 2

# WHAT IS AN ANNUAL REPORT?

The key to understanding an annual report is to realize that it is designed to satisfy the information needs of many different people with many different needs. Stockholders, creditors, potential stockholders, potential creditors, economists, financial analysts, suppliers, and customers all look to the same published annual report to satisfy their information needs.

The heart of an annual report is the financial statements, which must conform to accounting and reporting standards established by the Financial Accounting Standards Board (FASB), the Securities and Exchange Commission (SEC), and various committees of the American Institute of Certified Public Accountants (AICPA). The requirements of these different groups are a mixed blessing. Because financial statements are very structured, by both convention and legal requirements, they are not tailored to meet the needs of any one group precisely. Each group of users may find something lacking. But because of the high degree of structure and the involvement of the Certified Public Accountant (CPA), readers of financial statements can rely on the fair presentation of the information they receive. Thus, we can review the financial statements of a company in New York or California and decide to buy stock, to lend money, or in some other way to become involved with the company, when we do not know any of the managers and have never seen the company's factory. Of course, there is always the possibility of outright fraud. Even experienced auditors can be fooled by unscrupulous operators.

A large company may spend over half a million dollars to have an independent CPA audit the financial statements, and another fortune to have the assembled, complete annual report published electronically on its Web site and on glossy paper for distribution to its shareholders. Designing and printing annual reports, with all their pictures and graphs and colors has become an industry in itself. Of course, the best-looking reports are not always the most informative reports. This book will help you distinguish the pertinent facts from the glossy presentation.

Most of this book will be concerned with explaining the keys to understanding the various facets of the financial statements. The next few sections, however, will focus on the contents of the annual report other than the accounting requirements of the financial statements.

# 3

# HIGHLIGHTS, LETTER, AND MANAGEMENT'S DISCUSSION AND ANALYSIS

When you pick up an annual report and begin to page through it, you will notice that the financial statements (the dull-looking pages) are toward the back. The front pages of an annual report, in contrast, are frequently beautiful, with full-color artwork and photographs. It is this glossy part of the report that management controls; accountants control the drab, rear portion. Management's part of the annual report typically consists of three sections and one report required by the Sarbanes-Oxley Act.

**1. Annual Report Highlights.** This section contains highlights of the company's operations, financial statements, stock performance, or whatever else management wishes to present. This section frequently includes graphs or tables to display the favorable trends management wishes to publicize. Generally, this section will also contain statements of the company's sales, profits, and earnings per share for several years. As you read through the keys on the following pages, you will become familiar with most of the terms and concepts introduced in the highlights.

**2. Letter to Shareholders.** "I am pleased to report (or inform or otherwise convey) . . ." is a common beginning for this section. The letter is from the president or both the president and the chairman of the board, and usually his or her (or their) smiling photograph accompanies the letter. The key to understanding the letter to shareholders is to ask "What do I expect them to say?" and "What did they really say?" The letter will contain the self-congratulatory, optimistic message you expect. That much is usually obvious. But it can be difficult to figure out what they are really saying. Vague wording, colorful adjectives, and meaningless euphemisms are frequently used to conceal the fact that, in truth, the managers are not telling you anything at all.

**3. Management's Discussion and Analysis.** This is where management discusses and analyzes the company's performance. Management's Discussion and Analysis is required by the Securities and Exchange Commission and, thus, should entail information without the public relations bias. Here, management is required to offer candid discussions that cover three areas: the company's results of operations, the adequacy of both liquid capital resources (short-term resources easily converted to cash), and capital (long-term) resources needed to fund operations. In addition, management is required to discuss all past and future conditions and uncertainties that may materially affect the business.

**4. Report Required by the Sarbanes-Oxley Act.** This report contains management's objective assessment of the effectiveness of the company's system of internal control over financial reporting.

# 4

# FINANCIAL STATEMENTS AND NOTES

At the heart of an annual report are the financial statements. The minimum report consists of a balance sheet, income statement, statement of cash flows, and the accompanying notes, report of Management Responsibilities and the auditor's opinion. All of these sections are analyzed in subsequent keys. The notes are often as important and informative as the statements themselves. These notes are largely descriptive and include information on such things as accounting methods, commitments, noncurrent liabilities and their due dates, inventory components, employee pension provisions, and a number of other disclosures.

In their report of responsibilities, management takes primary responsibility for the fairness, accuracy and completeness of the information included in the financial statements. This report also includes a short discussion of controls management put in place to provide assurance that the financial statements are accurate. This report is illustrated in Key 12.

The independent auditor's opinion is a short report addressed to the shareholders of the company, giving the auditor's opinion on the financial statements prepared by management. An unqualified opinion is good. Any other opinion is less than good. Qualified opinions, which contain the phrase "except for," should put you on guard. The entire auditor's opinion and a discussion of the types of opinions an auditor can give are discussed in Key 13.

The separate reports of the independent auditor and management on the effectiveness of the system of internal control over financial reporting are discussed in Key 14.

A number of supplementary tables may accompany an annual report, including:

- Reporting by divisions or other principal segments of the business
- Financial reporting and changing prices
- Five-year summary of operations
- Summary of quarterly figures for current and previous year

# 5

# ANNUAL REPORTS ON THE INTERNET

You can obtain a company's annual report by contacting the company directly via letter, telephone or the Internet. Many companies have an online version of their Annual Report and SEC filings. Company Web sites can be located using a search engine such as Google or Yahoo! These companies offer a link to their annual report on their Web site. Alternatively, annual report services make it convenient to order reports online (see below) and many sites provide digital annual reports that you can view online or download.

Annual reports on the Internet are often available in PDF using the Adobe Acrobat format, which only the Adobe Acrobat reader software can read. Most sites that use the Adobe Acrobat format include a link for downloading the reader software free. Several online sites that offer annual reports, SEC filings, or annual report services follow.

The **Report Gallery**, found on the Internet at *www.reportgallery.com*, calls itself "the most complete and up-to-date listing of Annual Reports online." The Report Gallery is a division of IR Solutions, a company that publishes financial data online.

You can choose among several options for obtaining information:

- *Company Name*: Type in the name of the company whose report you are interested in obtaining.
- *Ticker Symbol*: Type in the company's stock ticker symbol.

9

- *Exchange*: Click on the drop-down exchange menu, and click on a stock exchange. You will then be taken to a list of companies traded on that exchange. You may select a company of interest from that list.
- *Industry*: Clicking on the drop-down menu in this box takes you to a listing of industries. If you click on an industry of interest, you will be taken to a list of companies within that industry. You may select a company of interest for that list. Similarly, you may search by sector of the economy or alphabetically.

The **Public Register's Annual Report Service**, found at *http://www.prars.com/*, lets you request an annual report. Your request will be processed within 24 hours and the report shipped to you free of charge. You are limited to 8 requests per order. You may locate the reports you wish to order by entering either the company's stock ticker symbol or searching the alphabetic listing for the company's name. Once you have located the company you are interested in, click on the report you want from the list provided and then click "Add to Cart." When you have selected all the reports you want, click "Checkout," fill out the basic mailing information, and then click "Submit."

The SEC's **EDGAR** system, located under the "Filings & Forms" tab at *http://www.sec.gov/*, allows you to search for the SEC filings of publicly held companies. The primary purpose of the EDGAR system is to assist investors and others by making filings publicly available. Public availability of securities filings helps disseminate time-sensitive corporate information and is believed to increase the efficiency and fairness of the securities market. The Web site contains a tutorial for using EDGAR. Clicking on "Search for Company Filings" will bring up a page from which you may initiate either general-purpose or special-purpose searches. A general-purpose search of "Companies and Other Filers" will contain, among other information, SEC

Forms 10-K, 10-Q, and 8-K (see Key 16 for a discussion of SEC filings). Reports are available from 1994 onward.

Another useful site on the Internet is *http://www.marketwatch.com/tools/quotes/lookup.asp.* At this site, you may enter a company's name and obtain its stock ticker symbol. Alternatively, if you enter a stock ticker symbol, you will obtain the name of the company it represents. Searching the annual report Web sites mentioned above is most efficient if you use the stock ticker symbol rather than the company name.

# 6

# BASIC ACCOUNTING PRINCIPLES

Basic accounting principles are the rules and assumptions that underlie financial reporting. These principles tell accountants what items to measure and when and how to measure them. The basic accounting principles can be categorized as follows: (1) the accounting entity, (2) measurement of resources and obligations, (3) periodicity, (4) historical cost and unit of measure, (5) accrual, (6) substance versus form, (7) conservatism, and (8) materiality. The first seven of these concepts are defined and discussed below. Materiality is discussed in the next Key.

**Accounting Entity.** The accounting entity is the business unit for which financial statements are being prepared. Corporations and trusts are granted general legal existence separate from their owners, while proprietorships and partnerships are legally an extension of the owners' personal affairs. However, even in these latter two cases, accountants view the personal affairs of the owners as separate from the business. For unless each business unit is viewed separately, it is impossible to determine if a commercial venture has been profitable. An accounting entity may also be composed of a parent company and its majority-owned subsidiaries.

**Measurement of Resources and Obligations.** Business resources are those things of value that the business possesses and can use to produce a profit. The accounting term for resources is *assets*. Obligations, or *liabilities*, are amounts owed to nonowners of the business. The difference between assets and liabilities is the owners' interest (*equity*) in the business. This sum includes their personal investment (*contributed capital*) plus any profits earned by the business and not paid out to the owners (*retained earnings*). A set of financial statements contains measures of assets, liabilities, and owners' equity at the end of the fiscal period (in the balance sheet), and changes that have occurred in assets, liabilities, and owners' equity during the period (in the income statement, statement of retained earnings, and statement of cash flows).

**Periodicity.** This is the assumption that a company's life must be divided into periods of time in order to measure profit or loss. Ultimately, we can only determine profitability by comparing the owner's interest at the time the business began to their interest at the time of dissolution. Viewing profit or loss at the end of the business's life does not provide timely information for management, investment, or credit decisions. Therefore, accountants divide a company's life into fiscal periods— for example, fiscal year or a fiscal quarter.

**Historical Cost and Unit of Measure.** This is another measurement concept. Assets and liabilities are recorded in the accounting records at their original or historical cost. For example, if we purchase land for $1 million with a $1 million mortgage, the assets would be increased by $1 million (the land) and the liabilities would be increased by $1 million (the mortgage note). These values will continue in the accounting records until another business event indicates the need for changing them. Examples of such events would include the sale of an asset, the payment of a liability, or the ability to repurchase an asset at less than its historical cost.

The unit of measure employed in financial statements of U.S.-based entities is the nominal dollar, unadjusted for inflation or deflation. As a result, one company may have land acquired in 1960 on its books at $100,000, while another company may have a similar piece of property acquired in 1998 recorded on its books at $1 million.

13

**Accrual.** The accrual principle attempts to translate into dollars of profit or loss the actual activities of the fiscal period. The accrual principle is a combination of two ideas:

The *revenue recognition* principle provides that revenue (sales price) be recorded when the necessary activities to sell a good or provide a service have been completed. Revenue is recorded at the point of sale regardless of whether cash is collected or a receivable from the customer is created.

The *matching* principle tells the accountant when to record a production cost as expense.

Costs directly associated with producing a certain revenue will be expensed in the same period that the revenue is recorded as earned. Sales commissions are an example of this type of cost because there is a direct association between the sale and the effort of the salesperson.

Other costs are long-lived. They help produce revenue for several periods. Examples include the cost of plant and equipment. The accountant expenses the cost of these types of assets over their expected lives. If a piece of equipment is expected to be used for ten years, its historical cost should be expensed as a cost of revenue production over that same period. This is depreciation (Key 22).

Other costs are expensed when they arise. These are costs that would not be expected to produce future sales— for example, the cost of heating or cooling a factory.

Under the matching principle an expense can be recorded before, after, or at the time a cost is actually paid. From the accountant's point of view it is the earnings activity that gives rise to the conversion of cost to expense—it does not matter whether that cost has been paid or a liability created.

**Substance Versus Form.** The accountant attempts to report the economic substance of a transaction without regard to its form. For instance, a pledge to United Way is not really a legally binding obligation on the company, but an accountant would record it as a liability. Why? Because the substance of the transaction is that management intends to pay the pledge. The company has made a promise. Its reputation is on the line. Avoiding payment without damaging its reputation is unlikely. The company will choose to pay the pledge.

**Conservatism.** Conservatism is a downward measurement bias, preferring undervaluation to overvaluation, understatement of income to overstatement of income. The accounting practice of conservatism favors continuing to value assets at their historical cost even though the asset (perhaps land) may be increasing in value each year. Conservatism favors recording losses even before they actually occur if they are considered "likely" to occur. However, the recording of a gain will be postponed until the gain actually occurs even when the gain is considered "likely" to occur (see discussion of contingencies in Key 9).

# 7
# MATERIALITY

Materiality deals with relative importance. Considerations of materiality pose the question: Could this item make a difference to the user of the financial statements? A transaction must be accounted for within the measurement and reporting principles known as Generally Accepted Accounting Principles (GAAP; see Key 13) when the amounts involved are judged to be material.

Materiality must be determined by the effect of the transaction on a company's financial statements. When pooled together, as they would be reported in the financial statements, similar transactions involving immaterial amounts may have a material effect. For instance, a large company's purchase of a single microcomputer costing $1500 is not material. Readers of the financial statements may not care if it is expensed or recorded as an asset. But what about 500 microcomputers, purchased at different times during the year? It would be misleading to treat this $750,000 purchase of office equipment as expense in the year of purchase. The computers have a useful life of more than one year and will benefit the company over their useful life. The combined amount of the purchases is material.

The Securities and Exchange Commission (SEC) has scolded accountants for misusing the materiality concept. Often CPA firms use a materiality threshold of 3 to 5 percent of total assets or total revenues, judging that errors below this threshold are not material and that management need not commit the resources (generally labor time) to correct them.

The SEC believes that company managers, knowing how CPAs behave, may make multiple intentional errors to manage profits. Even a small difference in profits can make a large difference in a company's stock price if the few pennies change in earnings per share causes the company to meet Wall Street's expectations when otherwise it would have fallen short.

Another factor affecting materiality is the cost-to-benefit concept. This concept holds that, in business, the benefit of doing something should exceed its cost. In accounting, the cost-to-benefit concept means that accountants will not determine, say, a cost or expense if the cost of the calculation is greater than the benefit the information provides. For example, accountants generally do not determine the depreciation cost on equipment each day. To do so would cost more than the benefit of having the information. Depreciation per month or even per quarter or six months is generally adequate. (Admittedly, circumstances can exist where managers might benefit from depreciation cost per day on particular machines—perhaps for a special study or cost calculation—but generally this is not the case.)

In the not-too-distant past, the cost of detailed calculations was much greater than it is today because all accounting was done by hand. Correcting an error might mean erasing and recalculating pages of figures. Now, however, computers make the cost of changing accounting records inconsequential. Spread sheet and data base records can be changed or an error corrected with only trivial, immaterial cost. The SEC rightly feels that it is cost beneficial to correct even very small errors. Certainly, the 3 to 5 percent materiality threshold of the past is now too large.

# 8

# NOTE ONE

The notes to the financial statements are as important as, if not more important than, the statements themselves. Many times, numbers by themselves do not adequately express *material* information (information that would make a difference to the financial statement user—see Key 7). Notes to the financial statements are largely descriptive and include information on such things as accounting methods, commitments, lease obligations, contingencies, and significant events affecting the company between the end of the fiscal year and the issuance of the annual report. These and other facets of an annual report will be explained in detail as we dissect a typical report in the keys that follow.

Financial reports summarize business transactions in the form of numbers. In some instances, various methods of reporting the same type of transaction have developed. Because these different methods have become popular through use, accountants have had a hard time standardizing reports.

Accounting principles require that if a company has a choice of methods it must disclose the methods used. Most companies list the methods they use in the first note to the financial statements or in a separate section headed Accounting Policies or a similar title. For example, different accounting methods exist for valuing inventories and computing depreciation. Acceptable inventory methods include specific identification, FIFO, LIFO, average cost, and lower of cost or market (see Key 20 for an explanation of these methods). Acceptable depreciation methods include straight-line, units of production, sum-of-the-years' digits, and double-declining balance (see Key 22 for an explanation of these methods).

**Red Flags.** The choice of accounting methods directly affects how the balance sheet is valued and how net income is computed. For example, in the first year of a machine's life, if depreciation is computed on a straight-line basis, it will be less than if it were computed on a sum-of-the-years' digits basis. Since depreciation is essentially a deduction from reported income, the less depreciation, the more income. Conversely, the less depreciation, the more the value reported on the balance sheet for the machine. So both balance sheet and net income figures are directly affected by whatever method of depreciation is used.

Financial statements of a company are not directly comparable, year-to-year, unless the company consistently uses the same valuation methods. (Companies are required to disclose a change in accounting methods; see Key 35.) Direct comparison of financial statements of two different companies is not possible unless they have used the same accounting methods. Note one is very important because it tells us the methods used by the company to prepare its financial statements. As we look at other areas of the financial statements, we will illustrate the major valuation methods so that you can begin to get a feel for their effect on balance sheet valuation and the computation of net income.

# 9

# NOTES ON COMMITMENTS, INCLUDING LEASES AND CONTINGENT LIABILITIES

**Commitments.** Different types of commitments are entered into by a company. Some commitments directly affect the balance sheet at the time they occur. For example, borrowing $1 million would increase assets $1 million and liabilities by $1 million. But as-yet unexecuted commitments may not be recorded on the balance sheet because they will not have any substantial effect on the company's operations until some time in the future. An example would be a commitment to purchase 5 million parts from a supplier over the next five years. Regardless of whether or not the commitment is recorded on the balance sheet, the principle of materiality requires that the details of all significant commitments be disclosed in the notes to the financial statements.

Some of the common types of commitments disclosed in financial statements are long-term purchase arrangements, the terms of outstanding loans, agreements to refinance existing debt, lines of credit, lease arrangements, and details of employee pension plans (see Key 10). You should pay close attention to these arrangements. Some time in the future they may add to the company's debt structure and increase the amount of cash necessary to meet current obligations.

**Leases.** Leases are a type of commitment, as indicated above. Some noncancellable long-term leasing arrangements are viewed as alternative purchase and mortgage arrangements. A lease can allow the lessee (party leasing the asset) to retain the asset at the end of the lease. Another lease agreement may set lease payments to cover the purchase price of the asset plus provide the lessor (party providing the asset) with a reasonable return ("interest"). Still another lease may grant the lessee the right to use the asset the majority of its useful life. These leasing arrangements, called capital leases, transfer the risks of ownership to the lessee. Because accountants believe that the economic substance of this type of lease arrangement is the same as an outright purchase of capital assets, they disregard the form of transaction and require it to be recorded as a purchase (see Substance vs. Form in Key 6).

In reporting capital leases, the lessee will record "Property Subject to Capital Leases" as an asset and "Obligations Under Capital Leases" as a liability. The amount recorded as the "historical cost" of the leased asset and the lease obligation is the present value of the required lease payments. Since this is a long-term arrangement, the lease payments must allow the lessors to recover not only their investment in the leased property but a reasonable return—"interest." Deducting this interest from the lease payments gives the "present value" of those payments, which is the value that is recorded as the "historical cost" of both the leased asset and the lease obligation.

The lessee will amortize (see Key 24) the leased asset's historical cost over the term of the lease (or over the asset's economic life if the lessee will obtain ownership of the asset at the end of the lease term). Lease payments are divided between principal payments on the recorded lease obligation and interest expense, just as loan payments are divided between payments of principal and interest expense.

21

Short-term leases and leases that do not transfer the risks of ownership are called operating leases. In these arrangements, the lessees do not record the leased asset or obligation on their balance sheet. All lease payments are recorded as rent expense.

Care should be taken when comparing financial statements of companies that lease to the financial statements of companies that do not lease. All leases give the lessee the benefit of using an asset in exchange for payments at specified intervals. Regardless of whether accounting principles require the lease to be recorded on the balance sheet, the company has a resource to use and an obligation that must be met by cash payments. The financial statement note on leases will provide you with the significant details of lease arrangements and payment schedules. A note relating to leased assets is shown on the next page.

**Contingencies.** A contingency exists when the company stands to gain or lose because of a past transaction or event. The amount of gain or loss is "contingent," that is, dependent on another transaction or event. For example, a customer falls in a department store and files a lawsuit. The store owners are now in a contingency situation. The event giving rise to possible loss is the injury of the customer. The amount of loss (if any) will be determined in the future by settlement or court verdict.

All contingencies may be classified by likelihood of outcome: (1) likely to occur, (2) remote chance of occurrence, or (3) may possibly occur. If management, their lawyers, and their accountants believe there is only a remote chance of gain or loss, a contingency will not be disclosed. Where it is possible that a gain or loss will result, the contingency must be disclosed along with management's estimate of the range of possible gain or loss.

If a contingency is viewed as likely to result in a loss, it must be accrued (the loss is recorded along with an estimated amount of liability). If a single estimate of loss cannot be determined, the smallest amount in management's estimated loss range will be accrued. Footnote disclosures will describe the nature of the contingency and the estimated range of loss.

Contingencies that are likely to result in gain are disclosed but not accrued. This is the principle of conservatism at work. The nature of the gain contingency will be described in the notes to the financial statements.

Notes on contingencies should be evaluated with care. Contingency losses may be time-bombs waiting to blow apart a profitable company. Ask yourself the questions: What will be the impact on the company's cash flow if the possible or likely contingency loss comes to pass? Is the company's debt and liquidity structure capable of handling the loss?

At December 31, 2008, future minimum rental payments under capital and operating leases were as follows:

| Year Ending December 31, | Capital | Operating |
|---|---|---|
| 2009 | $2.5 | $ 63.7 |
| 2010 | 2.0 | 55.1 |
| 2011 | 1.7 | 45.9 |
| 2012 | .8 | 37.0 |
| 2013 | .4 | 32.8 |
| Later years | .9 | 63.7 |
| Total minimum lease payments | 8.3 | 298.2 |
| Less: Minimum sublease rental income | — | 19.7 |
| Net minimum lease payments | 8.3 | $278.5 |
| Less: Interest and executory costs | 1.2 | |
| Present value of net minimum lease payments | $7.1 | |

Rent expense for all operating leases totaled $91.5 in 2008 and $80.3 in 2007 and 2006.

23

# 10

# NOTES RELATING TO PENSION AND POST-RETIREMENT BENEFITS

The key to understanding the cost of employee pension and other post-retirement benefits is to realize that the accounting records reflect management's best guess as to what the cost will be. Pensions refer to actual payments that will be made to former employees in retirement. Other post-retirement benefits refer to insurance and health-care costs the company pays for retirees. Accountants attempt to measure the cost of these retirement benefits at the time the employee earns them, rather than when the employee actually receives them. Pension expense represents the amount of money management should invest at the end of the year to cover future pension payments that will be made to employees for this additional year's service.

Why is pension cost a best guess? All kinds of assumptions must be made to calculate the required annual investment. Some of these assumptions are: average years of service of an employee at retirement, salary of employee at retirement, number of years an employee is expected to live after retirement, and interest invested funds are expected to earn.

As estimates change, revisions must be made to pension cost. Rather than adjusting the current period's pension expense, these revisions will be spread over the current and future accounting periods. Management may choose to invest more or less than the current year's pension expense. If more, the excess funding is recorded in an asset account, Prepaid Pension Cost; if less, it is recorded in a liability account, Accrued Pension Cost.

The health of a pension plan can be judged only by referring to the balance sheet. Although the balance sheet shows prepayments or pension liabilities for the difference between the amount recognized currently as expense and the funds transferred to the trustee, it will also show the funding status of the plan. A plan is considered overfunded if the fair market value of the plan's assets (value of the trust investments) is greater than the projected benefit obligation (the company's best estimate of today's cost of the total pension liability). Overfunded plans will show the excess fair value of the plan's assets as a noncurrent asset on the balance sheet. An underfunded plan is one where the value of the trust investments is less than the company's best estimate of today's cost of the total pension liability. Underfunded plans will show the excess of the projected benefit obligation over the value of the trust assets as a liability. When companies create pension plans, they may give employees service credit for years already worked. This creates prior-service cost, which is expensed over the employees' work lives and which may be funded over a period as long as thirty years. The company that routinely funds less than the current year's pension expense may find itself in trouble down the road.

The following tables set forth the funded status of both the defined benefit pension and the post-retirement plans and also the amounts recognized in the Consolidated Balance Sheet. SFAS No. 158, adopted by the Company effective December 30, 2006, requires the recognition of the overfunded or underfunded status of a defined benefit and post-retirement plans as an asset or liability in the balance sheet, with changes in the funded status recorded through other comprehensive income. Accordingly, the amounts presented in the table below for 2006 and 2005 utilize different accounting methodologies. The related value of the plans' assets is determined using the fair market value.

| (Dollars in millions) | Pension Benefits | | Post-Retirement Plans | |
|---|---|---|---|---|
| | 2006 | 2005 | 2006 | 2005 |
| **CHANGE IN BENEFIT OBLIGATION:** | | | | |
| Benefit obligation at beginning of year | $141.0 | $126.5 | $ 8.0 | $ 9.4 |
| Service cost | 9.9 | 8.2 | — | 0.1 |
| Interest cost | 7.6 | 7.2 | 0.4 | 0.5 |
| Plan charge | — | 0.5 | (1.1) | (1.1) |
| Plan participants' contributions | — | — | 0.5 | 0.7 |
| Actuarial (gain) loss | (6.5) | 9.0 | (0.7) | (0.3) |
| Benefits paid | (9.5) | (10.4) | (1.2) | (1.3) |
| Benefit obligation at end of year | $142.5 | $141.0 | $ 5.9 | $ 8.0 |
| **CHANGE IN PLAN ASSETS:** | | | | |
| Fair value of plan assets at beginning of year | $ 96.7 | $ 83.0 | $ — | $ — |
| Actual return on plan assets | 12.6 | 12.4 | — | — |
| Employer contributions | 12.1 | 11.7 | 0.7 | 0.6 |
| Plan participants' contributions | — | — | 0.5 | 0.7 |
| Benefits paid | (9.5) | (10.4) | (1.2) | (1.3) |
| Fair value of plan assets at end of year | $111.9 | $ 96.7 | $ — | $ — |
| Unfunded status/Accrued benefit cost at end of year | $ (30.6) | $ (44.3) | $ (5.9) | $ (8.0) |
| Unrecognized prior service cost | — | 0.9 | — | (1.1) |
| Unrecognized net actuarial loss | — | 41.2 | — | 3.4 |
| Additional pension liability | — | (25.6) | — | — |
| Accrued benefit cost at end of year | $ (30.6) | $ (27.8) | $ (5.9) | $ (5.7) |
| **AMOUNTS RECOGNIZED IN THE CONSOLIDATED BALANCE SHEET:** | | | | |
| Other current liabilities | $ (0.2) | $ (8.8) | $ (0.4) | — |
| Other liabilities | (30.4) | (19.0) | (5.5) | (5.7) |
| Net amount recognized | $ (30.6) | $ (27.8) | $ (5.9) | $ (5.7) |

Notice that this note gives a brief description of the plan and indicates the employee groups covered, discusses management's funding policy, gives a breakdown of the current period's net pension expense, a reconciliation of the plan's funding status to the pension amounts in the balance sheet, and a summary of assumed interest rates used in the computations.

**Red Flags.** Don't get carried away trying to analyze this material. It is only best-guess information. Much of the reconciliation data is irrelevant if your purpose is to evaluate the health of the company's pension plans. Only three figures are relevant for that analysis: (1) fair value of the plan's assets (value of the trust investments), (2) the projected benefit obligation (the company's best estimate of the total pension liability), and (3) the difference between these two. If a company reports a liability because its projected benefit obligation is greater than the value of its pension investments, given the current rate of earnings, the company's pension fund investments are not enough to cover the future benefits that management expects to pay the employees. If the company reports an asset because the value of its pension investments exceeds its projected benefit obligation, it has a cushion. This is the case in our sample disclosure above, which shows an overfunded plan.

Like pension cost, the cost of retirement health care and other supplemental benefits must be estimated and expensed over the employee's worklife. Unlike pensions, many companies pay for these supplemental benefits as they go, choosing not to set up a trust fund. This means they must fund these benefits out of current operations! Disclosures similar to those provided for pension cost are in the notes to the financial statements.

27

# 11

# SEGMENTAL AND COMPANY-WIDE INFORMATION

When investors purchase a share of stock in a large corporation, frequently they are buying a share of a conglomerate—a parent company with subsidiaries in different lines of business. If you purchase a share of one major retailer, you are buying a share of retail, insurance, real estate, and computer information services operations! A question you might ask is, "How are the components of this company doing?" While the insurance market may be prospering, real estate may not be doing well.

FASB Statement No. 131 requires that companies report financial and some descriptive nonfinancial information about its operating segments. Operating segments are defined as "components of an enterprise about which separate financial information is available that is evaluated regularly by the chief operating decision maker in deciding how to allocate resources and in assessing performance." This means information should be reported the same way it is used internally for management decisions.

**Segment Information.** The company must report segment profit or loss, certain revenue and expense items, and each segment's assets. Segment revenues, profit (or loss), total assets, and other amounts disclosed in the financial statements must be reconciled to totals in the general-purpose financial statements.

Companies also are required to report information about:

28

1. the revenues from the enterprise's products or services (or groups of similar products and services);
2. the countries in which the enterprise earns revenues and holds assets; and
3. major customers.

**Descriptive Information.** The company must disclose descriptive information about:

1. the way that the operating segments were determined;
2. the products and services provided by the operating segments;
3. any differences between the measurements used in reporting segment information and in the enterprise's general purpose financial statements; and
4. any changes in the measurement of segment amounts from period to period.

Hopefully, understanding how the different segments of the company contribute to its overall performance will help investors make better judgments about the performance of the company as a whole, both its profit and its net cash flow.

An example of segmental disclosure taken from an annual report is shown below.

| | Fiscal Year Ended September 30, | | |
|---|---|---|---|
| | **2006** | **2005** | **2004** |
| **Net sales to unaffiliated customers:** | | | |
| Fire and emergency | $ 961,467 | $ 841,465 | $ 599,734 |
| Defense | 1,317,237 | 1,061,064 | 744,059 |
| Commercial | 1,190,323 | 1,085,700 | 907,309 |
| Intersegment | (41,639) | (28,329) | (18,797) |
| Consolidated | $3,427,388 | $2,959,900 | $2,262,305 |

Intersegment sales are primarily from the fire and emergency segment to the defense segment.

|  | Fiscal Year Ended September 30, | | |
| --- | --- | --- | --- |
|  | **2006** | **2005** | **2004** |
| **Operating income (expense):** | | | |
| Fire and emergency | $ 89,999 | $ 79,619 | $ 54,957 |
| Defense | 242,271 | 210,232 | 127,859 |
| Commercial | 66,179 | 23,829 | 34,838 |
| Corporate and other | (72,521) | (46,478) | (37,244) |
| Consolidated operating income | 325,928 | 267,202 | 180,410 |
| **Interest expense net of interest income** | (747) | (5,183) | (4,314) |
| **Miscellaneous other income (expense)** | (243) | (1,898) | 452 |
| **Income before provision for income taxes, equity in earnings of unconsolidated affiliates and minority interest** | $324,938 | $260,121 | $176,548 |

**Red Flags.** Because the company can adopt whatever method it chooses for determining operating segments, some investors say the standard allows management to manipulate the presentation of segment information. Additionally, the FASB standard designates a decision maker as being responsible for determining operating segments, which could conceivably be anyone—the financial director, the chief financial or operating officer, or the company board. Each, legitimately, might see the company differently.

Many have criticized the segment-reporting standard for requiring information in a format that reveals important information to competitors. The FASB may address this issue.

# 12

# MANAGEMENT EVALUATION OF DISCLOSURE CONTROLS AND PROCEDURES

The SEC requires companies to provide shareholders with a report on internal controls as part of Management's Report of Responsibilities. The Committee of Sponsoring Organizations (COSO) of the Treadway Commission[1] has provided guidance for nonpublic companies who issue reports on internal controls.

COSO has defined internal control as "a process, effected by an entity's board of directors, management, and other personnel, designed to provide reasonable assurance regarding achievement of objectives in the following categories:

- effectiveness and efficiency of operations;
- reliability of financial reporting; [and]
- compliance with applicable laws and regulations."

Within these three categories of objectives, COSO identified several components of control that should be considered by companies. Companies should examine their control environment with attention to the ethical values and operating style of top management. The "tone at the top" has a great impact on the way people behave throughout the organization. Companies should

---

[1] See the Committee of Sponsoring Organizations of the Treadway Commission, *Internal Control—Integrated Framework,* Reporting to External Parties, September 1992.

31

assess and control the risk related to operating activities, such as the risk of an employee embezzling funds or a vendor supplying substandard goods. Good internal control requires that important information be identified and communicated to managers and shareholders. Finally, internal control must be monitored to assure that it remains effective.

COSO recommends that reports on internal control address the following:

- the type of controls reported on (usually preparation of the company's published financial statements);
- the inherent limitations of control systems (stating that no control system can be expected to be perfect);
- the existence of procedures for monitoring controls and responding to control deficiencies;
- the criteria against which the control system is evaluated;
- a conclusion about the effectiveness of the control system and a description of any weaknesses.

Management's formal report on the effectiveness of internal control over financial reporting as required by the Sarbanes-Oxley Act is found in Key 14.

# 13

---

# AUDIT REPORTS

A sample audit report for a publicly held company follows.

### Report of Independent Registered Public Accounting Firm on Financial Statements

The Board of Directors and Shareowners
of Coca-Cola Enterprises, Inc.

We have audited the accompanying consolidated balance sheets of Coca-Cola Enterprises, Inc. as of December 31, 2006 and 2005, and the related consolidated statements of operations, shareowners' equity, and cash flows for each of the three years in the period ended December 31, 2006. Our audits also included the financial statement schedule listed in the Index at Item 15(a). These financial statements and schedule are the responsibility of the Company's management. Our responsibility is to express an opinion on these financial statements and schedule based on our audits.

We conducted our audits in accordance with the standards of the Public Company Accounting Oversight Board (United States). Those standards require that we plan and perform the audit to obtain reasonable assurance about whether the financial statements are free of material misstatement. An audit includes examining, on a test basis, evidence supporting the amounts and disclosures in the financial statements. An audit also includes assessing the accounting principles used and significant estimates made by management as well as evaluating the overall financial statement presentation. We believe that our audits provide a reasonable basis for our opinion.

In our opinion, the consolidated financial statements referred to above present fairly, in all material respects, the consolidated financial position of Coca-Cola Enterprises, Inc. at December 31, 2006 and 2005, and the consolidated results of its operations and its cash flows for each of the three years in the period ended December 31, 2006, in conformity with U.S. generally accepted accounting principles. Also, in our opinion, the related financial statement schedule, when considered in relation to the basic financial statements taken as a whole, presents fairly in all material respects the information set forth therein.

As discussed in Notes 2, 9, 11, and 13, in 2006 the Company adopted Statement of Financial Accounting Standards ("SFAS") No. 123 (revised), "Share-Based Payment," and the recognition provisions of SFAS No. 158, "Employers' Accounting for Defined Benefit Pension and Other Postretirement Plans."

We have also audited, in accordance with the standards of the Public Company Accounting Oversight Board (United States), the effectiveness of Coca-Cola Enterprises, Inc.'s internal control over financial reporting as of December 31, 2006, based on criteria established in Internal Control—Integrated Framework issued by the Committee of Sponsoring Organizations of the Treadway Commission, and our report dated February 13, 2007, expressed an unqualified opinion thereon.

/s/ Ernst & Young LLP

Atlanta, Georgia
February 13, 2007

The audit report form is designed to increase public awareness of the nature and limitations of the audit. As stated in the first paragraph of the report, management (not the auditors) is primarily responsible for the financial statements.

The second paragraph of the audit report describes just what an audit is. The auditor tests the accounting records and supporting documents to form an opinion on the reasonableness of the financial statements. Standards developed by the SEC's Public Company Accounting Oversight Board (PCAOB) offer guidance and define the auditor's responsibilities in various situations. For instance, the standards require that the auditor confirm receivables and payables. In order to do this the auditor draws only test samples of these items.

The third paragraph of the audit report contains the auditors' opinion. Auditors may express a "clean," "qualified," or "adverse" opinion, or they may "disclaim" and express no opinion at all. The report quoted above expresses a clean opinion. Based on their tests, the auditors believe the financial statements are "fair" presentations of the company's financial position and earnings for the year.

The auditors also state that the financial statements are "in conformity with generally accepted accounting principles" (GAAP), the accounting profession's collection of rules and basic principles governing financial statement presentation and measurement. (See Key 6.)

A qualified opinion takes exception to "fair presentation" and points out the particular area(s) that the auditors do not believe to be "fair presentation." It is implicit that the auditors believe the remainder of the statements to be fairly presented.

An adverse opinion states that the auditors do not believe the financial statements are "fairly presented." When the auditors issue such an opinion, they will list the factors that led them to this opinion.

This example audit report has two additional paragraphs. The fourth paragraph emphasizes changes in accounting principles that were made during the fiscal year. These changes and their effect on the financial statements are explained in the specific notes to the financial statements indicated in the audit report.

In the fifth paragraph, the auditors express an opinion about management's system of internal controls over financial reporting. This opinion is required for publicly-held companies and may be combined with the audit report on financial statements or issued as a self-standing report. Like the audit report on the fairness of presentation of the financial statements, the opinion about management's system of internal controls over financial reporting can be clean (unqualified), qualified (except for), or adverse (management's controls are not adequate to insure the integrity of the financial reporting process). For more about internal controls, see Key 14.

**Red Flag.** The auditors base their opinion of the financial statements on the evidence they gather from the test samples. Because this is far from a complete test of the accounting records, material misstatement may exist without the auditors being aware of it.

# 14

# REPORTS REQUIRED BY SARBANES-OXLEY

Not long after the stock markets rocked to the corporate financial scandals of Enron, Tyco, and WorldCom, Congressmen Paul Sarbanes and Michael G. Oxley sponsored and Congress passed the Sarbanes-Oxley Act, commonly known as SOX or Sarbox.

The legislation (a) prohibited several questionable activities and (b) increased the transparency of corporate financial reporting. Prohibited acts included some types of insider trading, all personal loans to executive officers and directors, and certain nonaudit work by a company's auditors that were felt to create a conflict of interest. The act increased transparency by requiring a number of new or beefed-up disclosures, including insider trading and both CEO and CFO compensation. SOX increased penalties for violations of securities laws and intentionally misstating financial statements.

Most important perhaps, Accounting Standard No. 2 (AS2), "An Audit of Internal Control over Financial Reporting Performed in Conjunction with an Audit of Financial Statements," now requires publicly traded companies to include two new reports in their financial statements:

1. management's assessment of the effectiveness of the company's internal control over financial reporting; and
2. the company's outside auditor's report on management's assessment of internal control over financial reporting.

"Internal control" refers to all the measures management puts into place to assure that information is gathered, recorded, and reported accurately and that assets are protected. For example, management may require bank statements to be reconciled by a person outside the financial function to confirm the accuracy of the cash transactions recorded and two signatures on a check to protect assets.

**Management's Report.** Unlike management's representations in other portions of the annual report, AS2 requires that management not prepare a public relations report but instead provide a direct, objective conclusion about the effectiveness of the company's internal control. AS2 suggests managers use phrases such as:

> [The] Company maintained effective internal control over financial reporting as of [date].

AS2 prohibits subjective assessments such as "very effective internal control" that statement readers could define in different ways. After reading that subjective statement, one reader may think the controls are very effective while another may think they are marginally effective. A cat is either dead or alive, not somewhat dead or very dead. Similarly, internal controls are either effective or not effective.

Provision has been made for management to assert that internal controls over financial reporting are effective as of the end of the year, even if material weaknesses were present during the year. The report may use a phrase such as:

> [The] Company's internal control over financial reporting as of [date] is sufficient to meet the stated objectives.

**The Auditor's Report.** The company's outside auditors must assess two aspects of internal control, either in separate reports or in one combined report. They must provide their opinion on management's assessment of the effectiveness of internal controls over financial reporting and, separately, their opinion on the effectiveness of the company's system of internal controls.

Because they rely on internal controls during the performance of their audit, auditors are required to examine internal controls as part of the preliminary survey. Howver, before AS2, external auditors were not required to express an explicit opinion on the controls

Although the report on internal controls was new for auditors, the basic work on which it is based is not. In contrast, the auditor's opinion on management's assessment of internal controls is new. AS2 requires the auditors to examine a number of things before forming an opinion.

1. Has management properly stated that establishing and maintaining adequate internal control is management's responsibility (not the accountants')?
2. Has management used a suitable framework to conduct its evaluation of the control system?
3. Is management's assessment of control effectiveness free of material misstatement?
4. Has management disclosed all material weaknesses identified, even those corrected before year end? (Management cannot assert that internal control is effective if even one material weakness remains.)
5. Is management's assessment in an acceptable form? (Management is not permitted to give negative assurance, such as, "Nothing has come to management's attention to suggest that the company's internal control over financial reporting is not effective.")

An example of the auditor's report on internal control is shown in Key 13.

# 15

# COMPILATION AND REVIEW REPORTS

Occasionally you may run across a set of financial statements that have been *reviewed* or *compiled*. These types of services are performed by a CPA but do not carry the same weight as an audit, which results in the CPA's issuing an opinion on the fairness of financial statement presentation, as described in Key 13. Because of time and cost considerations, quarterly financial statements are reviewed rather than audited. Businesses that do not regularly make their financial statements available to the public may prefer reviews or compilations to the audit because of cost considerations.

**Reviews.** A review consists of two basic techniques, making inquiries and performing analytical procedures.

**Auditor inquiries** consist primarily of questions regarding:

1. procedures for recording, classifying, and summarizing transactions and for accumulating information to be included in the financial statements (see Key 14 for an explanation of internal controls); and
2. who is responsible for making decisions and taking action on accounting matters.

**Analytical procedures** require the CPA to examine the relationships in the accounts that would be expected to follow a predictable pattern. For example, if in past years, the company has held inventories equal to 40 percent of one month's sales, the CPA would expect the same relationship to continue this year unless management changed its policy for some reasons. The CPA would compare this year's actual results with the expected pattern and investigate amounts that deviated. For example, if inventories this year were 60 percent of sales, the auditor would ask managers to explain the change. Was there fraud, reducing the level of recorded sales, or an error in inventory records? Or did managers simply decide higher inventory levels were necessary? Where relationships appear normal the CPA does not investigate further.

The following examples of differences in audit procedures and review procedures should help you to understand the basic difference between them. In an audit, a CPA would be present at the counting of year-end inventories. In a review, the CPA would merely perform an analytical review and ask questions about the procedures used to count inventories. Auditing standards require the CPA to obtain written confirmations from customers of the amounts they owe the company in order to evaluate accounts receivable. Written confirmations are also obtained from suppliers indicating the amounts owed by the business, in order to evaluate accounts payable. The CPA would not perform such procedures in a review but would review relationships and ask: Have all sales and payments from customers been recorded? Have all purchases and payments to suppliers been recorded?

In a review report, CPAs must state that they are not aware of any material changes needed to make the financial statements conform to Generally Accepted Accounting Principles (GAAP). CPAs also must state that they have not audited the financial statements and are not expressing an opinion on their fairness of presentation.

**Compilations.** In a compilation the CPA reads the financial statements and decides whether they are in proper form and appear to contain appropriate disclosures. The CPA also checks the mathematics of the statements. For instance, in examining the balance sheet: Do assets equal liabilities plus owners' equity? CPAs are not required to analyze relationships or to ask management questions about the preparation of the statements. But their reports must state that they have not audited the financial statements and are not expressing an opinion on fairness of presentation.

When preparing financial statements not to be used or seen by a third party (anyone outside the company), a CPA may submit them without a standard compilation report as long as the CPA documents an understanding with the client.

**Unassociated Statements.** If a CPA finds a client is including the CPA's name in a letter or in other material accompanying financial statements prepared solely by the client, the CPA will be concerned that the recipient of the material may think the CPA is repsonsible for the accuracy of the statements and will require the client to include wording disavowing the CPA's association with the statements. That statement would resemble the following:

> The accompanying financial statement of BlueTone Foods as of March 31, 2008, were not audited, reviewed, or compiled by us and, accordingly, we do not express an opinion or any other form of assurance on them.
>
> —Tuttle and White, CPA

# 16

# SEC FORMS 10-K, 10-Q, AND 8-K

Part of the job of the Securities and Exchange Commission (SEC) is to ensure that current and potential investors and creditors have equal access to information about companies whose securities are publicly traded. The SEC accomplishes this task by requiring publicly held companies to file information periodically.

The SEC determines what information should be filed and how it should be presented, in addition to acting as a kind of clearinghouse for the reports. The major SEC-required forms are the 10-K (annual), 10-Q (quarterly), and 8-K (for significant changes). This information is on file at SEC offices and may be obtained over the Internet or as hard copy from a number of sources (see Key 5).

**Form 10-K.** This form must be filed with the SEC annually by publicly traded companies. The filing deadline is 60 days after the close of the company's fiscal year. Form 10-K contains essentially the same information that companies include in their annual reports, but in more detail. Additional information is also required to complete the 10-K. Sometimes a company will issue a combined annual report and 10K. This is allowed under the SEC's integrated disclosure rules.

The 10-K is divided into four parts, and each part is subdivided into individual items. Where information has been provided elsewhere, the company may reference those sources rather than duplicating the information.

# Form 10-K: Contents
## Part 1
1. Description of the company's business, including information on different segments of the company (for example, product lines, industries, domestic and foreign operations, or major classes of customers).
2. Description of the company's property.
3. Description of the legal proceedings in which the company is involved.
4. Discussion of matters that have been voted on by the shareholders.

## Part 2
5. Description of the market for the company's common stock including disclosures of: the principal U.S. markets on which the company's common stock is traded, quarterly high and low stock prices for the last two years, approximate number of shareholders, amount and frequency of cash dividends paid in the last two years, and any restrictions on the company's ability to pay dividends.
6. Five-year summary of selected financial data, including net sales (operating revenues), income or loss from continuing operations, income or loss from continuing operations per common share, total assets, long-term debt and redeemable preferred stock, and cash dividends per common share.
7. Management's discussion of the company's financial condition, changes that have occurred in financial condition, and results of operations. This discussion will include management's analysis of the company's liquidity, resources, and operations, the impact of inflation, the cause of major changes in the financial statements that have occurred during the year, and any material contingencies.
8. Financial statements, supplementary data, and auditor's report.
9. Changes in accounting principles and disagreements with the company's auditors.

## Part 3

10. List of directors and executive officers.
11. Compensation of the executive officers.
12. Company securities owned by management and major stockholders.
13. Information on related-party transactions, including transactions between the company and management, its subsidiaries, and major stockholders.
14. For the last 2 years:
    - audit fees,
    - audit-related fees,
    - tax fees, and
    - all other fees billed the company by the audit firm.

## Part 4

15. Exhibits, financial statement schedules, reports on Form 8-K.

**Form 10-Q.** This form is filed by a publicly traded company with the SEC at the end of each of its first three quarters of the fiscal year. The filing deadline is 40 days after the end of the quarter. Form 10-Q contains only quarterly information. The quarterly financial statements contained in the 10-Q have not been audited, only reviewed by the company's CPAs (see Key 14).

**Form 8-K.** This form is used to report any significant changes that have occurred in the information the company has filed with the SEC. Form 8-K does not contain audited data. Some of the changes reported on Form 8K are changes in the company's controlling interest, major purchases or sales of assets, filing for bankruptcy or receivership, a change of the company's auditors, and resignations of directors. Filing of the 8-K must take place within 4 days of a significant change.

# 17

# COMPONENTS OF THE BALANCE SHEET

Accountants use a system of record keeping called double-entry bookkeeping. This system is based on the relationship between business resources and the source of those resources. Business resources are called assets and may be obtained either by borrowing (a liability) or by investment by the owners (equity). The relationship between assets, liabilities, and owners' equity can be expressed as:

$$\text{Assets} = \text{Liabilities} + \text{Owners' Equity}$$

If $10,000 of resources are contributed by investors, both assets and equity will be increased by the same amount, $10,000. If $5000 cash is borrowed from the bank, both assets and liabilities will be increased by $5000. Thus, after each transaction is recorded, assets will still equal liabilities plus owners' equity.

A balance sheet is a report that displays the assets, liabilities, and owners' equity of a business as of a specific date. The recorded value of the assets will equal the recorded value of the liabilities plus owners' equity. An alternative name for the balance sheet is Statement of Financial Position.

**Assets.** Those things of value that the business possesses and can use as it attempts to produce a profit are called assets. In order for a company to record an asset on its balance sheet, the resource must possess three characteristics: (1) positive potential cash flow, (2) the ability to be controlled, and (3) the right of use or control, granted in a past transaction or event.

The first characteristic, positive potential cash flow, means that management believes that the resource is capable of bringing more cash into the business than will flow out of the business as the result of using the resource. The purchase of a fleet of delivery trucks, for example, will enable a company to deliver more of its own products to customers in less time, thus increasing its sales. The second characteristic, control, indicates that the resource provides a competitive advantage that can be used as the company sees fit. With the trucks, the company can control its own delivery schedules. The third characteristic reflects the historical nature of accounting. Financial statements only report the results of past transactions or events. Thus, the trucks are first recorded as assets in the period when they were purchased.

In order to be listed as an asset on the balance sheet, a resource must not only possess these three characteristics but must also be capable of being valued. Significant resources often go unrecorded. For instance, employees are the most important resource many businesses have. But, how do you measure and objectively value an employee? You can't! Even though an employee could be considered an asset, valuation problems will prevent them from being listed as such.

Legal ownership is not a required characteristic of an asset. Equipment leased on a long-term lease that transfers the basic rights and risks of ownership will be recorded as an asset on the books of the company leasing the equipment (see Key 9).

**Liabilities.** The debts of the business—the amounts owed to nonowners—are its liabilities. These possess three major characteristics: (1) they represent the possibility of a future payment of cash to settle the obligation, (2) management has little chance of avoiding the obligation, and (3) the obligation arose in a past transaction or event.

Obligations do not have to be legally binding before they are recorded as a liability on the balance sheet. As noted previously, a pledge to United Way is not legally binding on management, but it will be recorded as a liability. Why? All three characteristics of a liability are present, and the obligation can be valued. The obligation exists as a result of management signing a pledge card (a past transaction or event). There exists the possibility of a future payment of cash to settle the pledge. And to avoid payment would damage the business's reputation.

**Owners' Equity.** Also called shareholders' equity, owners' equity in a corporation is the difference between the recorded values of the assets and of the liabilities. It includes amounts directly invested by the owners (contributed capital) plus any profits earned by the business that have not been paid out to the owners (retained earnings).

When a company realizes net income, the inflow of assets from revenues has exceeded the outflow of assets to produce those earnings. Since assets have increased and liabilities have not been affected, ownership must have increased. Retained earnings have thus grown.

A simple example will illustrate: Johnson invests $100,000 to begin a business. Immediately after his investment Johnson draws up the following balance sheet:

| ASSETS | | LIABILITIES | |
|---|---|---|---|
| Cash | $100,000 | | $       0 |
| | | OWNERS' EQUITY | |
| | | Contributed Capital | 100,000 |
| | $100,000 | | $ 100,000 |

Johnson pays $10,000 to buy inventory (an asset until it is resold). His balance sheet now appears as follows:

| ASSETS | | LIABILITIES | |
|---|---|---|---|
| Cash | $ 90,000 | | $       0 |
| Inventory | $ 10,000 | OWNERS' EQUITY | |
| | | Contributed Capital | 100,000 |
| | $100,000 | | $ 100,000 |

Johnson then sells merchandise that originally cost him $4500 (expense) for $6500 (revenue)—a net income of $2000. His balance sheet would appear as follows:

| ASSETS | | LIABILITIES | |
|--------|--------|--------|--------|
| Cash | $ 96,500 | | $      0 |
| Inventory | $   5,500 | OWNERS' EQUITY | |
| | | Contributed Capital | 100,000 |
| | | Retained Earnings | 2,000 |
| | $102,000 | | $ 102,000 |

**Classified Balance Sheet.** A classified balance sheet will generally contain the following categories:

| ASSETS | LIABILITIES |
|--------|-------------|
| Current Assets | Current Liabilities |
| Long-term | Long-term Liabilities |
| Investments | |
| Property, Plant and | |
| Equipment | |
| Intangibles | SHAREHOLDERS' EQUITY |
| Other Assets | Capital Stock |
| | Additional Paid-in Capital |
| | Retained Earnings |

Within each of these categories there are individual accounts. For example, current assets may include cash, short-term investments, receivables, inventories, and prepaid expenses. The categories and the individual accounts comprising a category will be discussed in the next 15 keys, which are illustrated with the various components of a full classified balance sheet.

**Red Flags.** The balance sheet is like a still photograph. It only shows resources, obligations, and equity at a point in time, typically the fiscal year-end. And, as you can see from our simple example above, each transaction affects the balance sheet, causing it to change immediately.

Assets and liabilities may go unrecorded because of measurement problems. Where such material information cannot be quantified, however, it will be reported in a note to the financial statements (see Keys 8, 9, and 10).

In some cases, items that meet the technical definition of an asset or liability are not reported on the face of the balance sheet because current accounting standards allow them to be reported in the notes. Where employers provide pensions for their employees, the invested assets are not recorded on the employers' books. The pension trust fund produces its own set of financial statements. Neither is the full pension obligation required to be reported as a liability on the face of the balance sheet (see Key 10). These obligations are quite real. While current rates of return on assets invested may be adequate to provide funds to meet these obligations, accountants do not forecast predictions about future earnings or the adequacy of investments to meet obligations in the future.

# 18

# CURRENT ASSETS

Current assets are short-term assets and are listed in a separate category in the balance sheet. Current assets are composed of cash, items that will provide cash, and certain items that will prevent the outflow of cash in the short term. The key to understanding the current assets category of the balance sheet is to examine the accountant's definition of current assets phrase by phrase.

Accountants define *short-term* as one year or one company operating cycle, whichever is greater. Thus, short-term may mean different time periods for different companies, depending on their operating cycles. A company's operating cycle is the length of time required to go "from cash to cash" in operations. To explain, cash is first invested in inventory, either by manufacturing something or by purchasing a product for resale. Next, the inventory is sold, creating an account receivable. Finally, the receivable is collected, and cash is put in the till, thus completing the cycle. The length of time a company's cash is tied up in accounts receivable and inventory can be estimated using the technique explained in Key 53.

Usually, cash is tied up 30 to 60 days in both accounts receivable and in inventories, and a company's operating cycle is anywhere from 60 to 120 days. As a result, the time span for current assets is most often one year. But some companies leave cash in inventories for a very long time. A whiskey distiller, for instance, may age inventory for 12 years during the manufacturing process. The operating cycle for such a distiller may then be the total of the 12 years cash is invested in inventory plus the 30 days cash is invested in receivables!

Current assets for such a distillery could thus include items that would provide cash in 12 years and 30 days. This would allow the distiller to include its inventory of aging whiskey as a current asset.

The types of assets classified as current assets include:

1. Cash.
2. Items that will provide cash in one year or one operating cycle, whichever is greater, including accounts receivable, short-term notes receivable, and inventories of raw materials, supplies, and finished goods.
3. Items that prevent the outflow of cash in one year or one operating cycle, whichever is greater, including prepaid insurance, prepaid rent, and employee advances.

A current assets section is shown below.

|  | 2009 | 2008 |
| --- | --- | --- |
| Cash and temporary cash investments | 84.4 | 89.6 |
| Accounts receivable (less allowance for doubtful accounts: 2009/$5.0 and 2008/$7.6) | 400.9 | 414.1 |
| Contract receivable (Note 3) | 94.6 | — |
| Materials, supplies, and fuel stock (at average cost) | 97.3 | 118.4 |
| Inventory | 72.9 | 87.2 |
| Prepayments | 21.9 | 16.0 |
| TOTAL CURRENT ASSETS | 772.0 | 725.3 |

**Red Flags.** Sometimes the term working capital is used to refer to current assets. But you must be alert. Working capital is also used to refer to net current assets—or current assets minus current liabilities. Long ago, net working capital was used to refer to net current assets, and working capital referred to current assets, but this distinction is now seldom made.

# 19

# CASH AND RECEIVABLES

**Cash.** The most active asset in a company's balance sheet is its cash. Few business transactions will occur that do not affect cash in some way, either providing cash or requiring it. Cash itself is a relatively unproductive asset (earning at best a nominal interest rate on time deposits), but it is vitally important to the day-to-day operations of a business. Cash is also the most universally desirable asset that a company possesses: it is easily transported, hard to recognize once off the company premises, and easily convertible into other goods. Cash is subject to more accounting and management controls than any other asset.

Cash includes only the most liquid current assets. To be reported as "cash," an item must be readily available for payment of current obligations. Items classified as cash include:

- coin and currency on hand
- petty cash funds
- checking accounts (unrestricted funds available on deposit in a bank)
- change funds (for cash registers, etc.)
- negotiable instruments (such as personal checks, travelers' checks, cashiers' checks, bank drafts, and money orders.)

Cash balances earmarked for some special purpose should not be reported as "cash." Examples of special-purpose cash balances include bond sinking funds or employee travel funds. Neither are readily available to meet current obligations. Special-purpose cash balances are reported in the balance sheet as "restricted funds." Similarly, certificates of deposit, money market funds, Treasury bills, and commercial paper are not readily available to meet current obligations. Still, these items are generally classified and reported as cash equivalents under current assets.

**Receivables.** All amounts owed to a company that are expected to be settled in cash are called receivables. The chief source of receivables is usually the company's regular trade customers. All receivables can be classified as either trade receivables or nontrade receivables. Trade receivables are mostly accounts or notes receivable. The most common type of receivable reported in the balance sheet, trade receivables also usually represent the largest dollar amount.

Nontrade receivables can be either current or noncurrent. Examples of nontrade receivables are accounts or notes receivable arising from the following types of transaction:

- claims for losses or damages
- claims for tax refunds
- dividends or interest receivable
- advances to employees
- sales of property other than inventory
- deposits with creditors or utilities

Receivables may appear in the current assets section of the balance sheet as illustrated below. Details as to allowances for doubtful accounts, when not shown on the face of the balance sheet, would be in Note One, Significant Accounting Policies.

Sample notes on cash and accounts receivable are shown below.

Note 8: *Cash and Marketable Securities*

| (*Millions of dollars*) | 2009 | 2008 |
|---|---|---|
| Cash | $ 9 | $ 8 |
| Time deposits | 95 | 34 |
| Certificates of deposit | 65 | 132 |
| Marketable securities | — | 7 |
| Total | $ 220 | $ 246 |

The marketable securities are stated at cost, which approximates market value.

Note 9: *Accounts Receivable, Net*

| (*Millions of dollars*) | 2009 | 2008 |
|---|---|---|
| Customers | $ 315 | $ 289 |
| Unconsolidated subsidiaries and affiliates | 16 | 10 |
| Employee | 4 | 3 |
| Other | 28 | 23 |
| | 363 | 325 |
| Less allowance for losses | 7 | 7 |
| Total | $ 356 | $ 318 |

**Red Flags.** Certain credit transactions may require the pledging or assignment of receivables as security for a loan. With a "general assignment," all accounts receivable serve as collateral. With a "specific assignment," specific accounts receivable may be pledged as collateral.

Notes receivable may be "discounted" to a bank. When notes receivable are discounted, the company receives immediate cash and the bank receives repayment when the note is collected. When notes receivable are discounted with recourse, the company will disclose any obligations on the discounted notes.

# 20

# INVENTORIES

There are several different types of inventory. For instance, a manufacturer may have inventories of raw materials, inventories of partially completed work in process, and inventories of supplies used in operations, in addition to an inventory of manufactured finished goods available for sale. And a retailer's inventory may consist only of purchased finished goods available for sale.

Inventories are current assets, carried in the balance sheet either at original historical cost, or at the lower of cost or market value. The cost of purchased goods in a retailer's inventory includes the cost of transportation or freight in, but is reduced by any purchase discounts taken by the buyer, any returns made, or any allowances received. A schedule of ending inventories for a retailer is illustrated below.

| SCHEDULE OF ENDING INVENTORIES | | |
|---|---:|---:|
| Beginning Inventory | | 75,000 |
| Purchases | 250,000 | |
| Plus: Freight-in | 10,000 | |
| Less: Purchase Discounts | (5,000) | |
| Returns and Allowances | (15,000) | |
| Net delivered cost of purchases | | 240,000 |
| Total goods available for sale | | 315,000 |
| Less: Cost of goods sold | | 255,000 |
| Ending inventory | | 60,000 |

The components of a manufacturer's inventories will be shown either in the body of the financial statements or in the statement notes. A schedule of inventory components for a manufacturer is illustrated below.

Note B—Inventories

Inventories are valued at cost not in excess of market, using the first-in, first-out (FIFO) method. The major components of inventory as of November 30 were as follows:

| (in thousands) | 2009 | 2008 |
|---|---|---|
| Raw materials | $49,751 | $19,753 |
| Work in-process | 4,662 | 2,945 |
| Finished goods | 20,254 | 11,713 |
| | $74,667 | $34,411 |

Since companies acquire inventories at different prices during the year, it is important to know the basis for inventory valuation. The method of inventory valuation is given in Note One of an annual report. The way inventories are valued affects both cost of goods sold and ending inventory; see Key 38.

Regardless of the inventory valuation method, inventories are usually shown on the balance sheet at the lower of historical cost or current market value. This prevents a company from carrying inventories at an inflated asset amount and forces a company to charge any loss in value against earnings in the period when the loss occurred. Without the lower-of-cost-or-market rule, inventories could be carried as current assets with an inflated value, and the loss (in value) would not be charged against earnings until the goods were sold, possibly in the year following the actual decline in inventory replacement prices. In most cases, managers would have an incentive to delay expensing the lost inventory value, in hopes market prices would rise again in the next year.

Finished-goods inventory turnover and days in inventory are discussed in Key 53. The turnover of both raw material and work-in-process inventories can also be calculated, although some of the figures needed may not be available in the company's annual report. There are four important formulas used in calculating turnover for all inventory components, as follows:

$$\text{Finished Goods Turnover} = \frac{\text{Cost of Goods Sold}}{\text{Average Finished Goods Inventory}}$$

$$\text{Work in Process Turnover} = \frac{\text{Cost of Goods Manufactured}}{\text{Average Work in Process Inventory}}$$

$$\text{Raw Material Turnover} = \frac{\text{Raw Material Used}}{\text{Average Raw Material Inventory}}$$

$$\text{Operating Supplies Turnover} = \frac{\text{Operating Supplies Used}}{\text{Average Operating Supplies Inventory}}$$

# 21

# PROPERTY, PLANT AND EQUIPMENT

The category of assets generally listed after Current Assets in the balance sheet is Property, Plant and Equipment. These are the company's long-lived productive assets—including land, buildings, furniture and fixtures, and machinery—and are carried at either their net historical cost less applicable depreciation, depletion, or amortization (see Key 22 and Key 24), or market value if lower. Just as with inventories, carrying at lower of net cost or market prevents overstatement of asset values. A note listing buildings, machinery, and equipment is shown on the next page.

The historical cost of a productive asset is the total cost connected with acquiring the asset and readying it for use. For example, the historical cost of a piece of machinery would include its invoice price, delivery charges, installation costs, and the cost of trial production runs to adjust the machine to the desired product quality. In other words, all costs incurred until the time production begins would generally be considered part of the machine's historical cost. Historical cost may also include interest cost on funds borrowed to finance the construction of plant and equipment.

The Property, Plant and Equipment line also generally includes the assets Leasehold Improvements and Property Subject to Capital Leases. The former is the cost of improvements made to leased property that will revert to its owner at the end of the lease term; the latter is property that has been acquired through a long-term leasing arrangement, which is essentially an alternative purchase and mortgage arrangement (see Key 9).

9. Buildings, machinery, and equipment at December 31, by major classification, were as follows:

|  | 2009 | 2008 | 2007 |
| --- | --- | --- | --- |
| Buildings | $2,076 | $2,071 | $2,068 |
| Machinery | 2,974 | 3,209 | 3,284 |
| Patterns, dies, jigs, etc. | 487 | 496 | 448 |
| Furniture and fixtures | 300 | 232 | 191 |
| Transportation equipment | 16 | 13 | 14 |
| Construction-in-process | 300 | 167 | 126 |
|  | 6,153 | 6,188 | 6,131 |
| Less acc. deprec. | 3,785 | 3,852 | 3,581 |
| Buildings, machinery, and equipment—net | $2,368 | $2,336 | $2,550 |

The company had commitments for the purchase or construction of capital assets of approximately $330 at December 31, 2009. Capital expenditure plans are subject to continuous monitoring and changes in such plans could reduce the amount committed.

**Red Flags.** Valuing at net historical cost, when it is lower than market value, causes problems in that it limits the usefulness of the figures obtained. Historical cost is an objective measure, but it may not be relevant to the decision maker. For instance, a piece of land valued at its 1940 historical cost of $1 million on a balance sheet tells us little about its current worth in terms of sales value or loan value. Comparisons between entities are also hampered by the use of historical cost—comparing the cost of property purchased in 1970 to the cost of similar property in 2008 is misleading. Although the 2008 property has a higher historical cost, it may not be any more productive than the 1970 property.

# 22

# DEPRECIATION

The key to understanding depreciation is to realize what accountants mean by the term. In ordinary usage, depreciation means decline in value. To the accountant, however, depreciation is the assignment of historical cost of a long-lived productive asset to production periods— the matching of costs of production (expenses) with the results of production (revenues). (Review the accrual concept as explained in Key 6, in particular the matching concept.) Rather than recording decline in value as depreciation, the accountant is recording the using-up of the original cost of the asset over its productive life.

The exception to the concept of depreciation is land, which is not used up. Land is a renewable resource. Therefore, land is not depreciated and is valued on the balance sheet at its historical cost, or market value if lower.

Companies generally use one (or a combination) of four primary depreciation methods in preparing their annual reports. These methods are (1) straight-line, (2) units of production, (3) sum-of-the-years' digits, and (4) double-declining balance. The depreciation methods used by a company will be disclosed in note 1, as shown below.

*Depreciation and Amortization*—Prior to July 1, 2008, substantially all of the Company's flight equipment was being depreciated on a straight-line basis to residual values (10% of cost) over a ten-year period from dates placed in service. As a result of a comprehensive review of its fleet plan, effective July 1, 2008, the Company increased the estimated useful lives of substantially all of its flight equipment. Flight equipment that was not already fully depreciated is now depreciated on a straight-line basis to residual values (10% of cost) over a 15-year period from dates placed in service. The effect of this change was a $130 million decrease in depreciation expense, and a $69 million ($1.54 per share) increase in net income, for the year ended June 30, 2009. Ground property and equipment are depreciated on a straight-line basis over their estimated service lives, which range from three to 30 years.

**Straight-line depreciation** assumes that equal benefit is derived from using the productive asset each year of its useful life. The formula for straight-line depreciation is:

Cost – salvage value/years of useful life = 1 year's depreciation

For example, if a company purchased a machine for $10,000 and at the time of purchase estimated its productive life to be three years, after which it would have a salvage value of $1,000, depreciation expense would be $3000 per year ($10,000 – $1000) /3.

**Units-of-production depreciation** assumes that revenue produced parallels units of product produced. In other words, in years in which more product is produced the company has greater revenue-producing ability. The formula for units-of-production depreciation is:

Cost – salvage value / units of product that can be produced over the life of the asset = per-unit depreciation

To find a year's depreciation expense we would multiply the number of units produced during the year by the per-unit depreciation rate. For example, assuming a cost of $10,000, a salvage value of $1000, a useful life of three years, and an estimated production of 4 million units of product over the three-year period, the depreciation rate per unit of product produced is [$10,000 – 1,000] / 4,000,000 = $.00225 per unit. If 1 million units are produced during the year, depreciation expense of $2250 would be recorded for the year (× .00225).

**Declining Balance Methods.** Both the sum of the years' digits and double-declining balance are declining balance methods of depreciation. They take more depreciation in the earlier years of an asset's life than in the later years. These methods assume that an asset is most productive (therefore, has the most revenue-producing ability) in the early years of the asset's life before wear and tear begin to take their toll.

The formula for the sum of the year's digits is:

Cost – salvage value × years in reverse order /
sum-of-the-year's digits

For a machine that has a $10,000 cost, $1000 salvage value, and a three-year life expectancy, the first year's depreciation expense would be calculated as follows: $10,000 – $1000 × 3/(1 + 2 + 3) = $9000 × 3/6 = $4500. The second year's depreciation expense would be ($9000 x 2/6) = $3000. The final year's depreciation would be ($9,000 × 1/ 6) = $1500. Notice that the rate of depreciation is declining year to year (1/2—1/3—1/6), not the depreciation base, which remains $9000.

The formula for double-declining balance depreciation is net book value of the depreciable asset × (2 / number of years estimated life).

Net book value of the depreciable asset—its original cost minus all depreciation taken to date (*accumulated depreciation*). Using our example of an asset that cost $10,000, with $1000 salvage value and a three-year estimated life, the first year's depreciation expense would be calculated as: ($10,000 – $0) × 2/3 = $6667. The second year's depreciation expense would be ($10,000 – $6667) × 2/3 = $2222.

The company will actually record only $111 of depreciation in the third and final year of the asset's life. This is the difference between net book value at the beginning of the third year and the estimated salvage value at the end of the third year ($10,000 – $8889) – $1000. The double-declining balance method is the only one of the four primary depreciation methods that ignores estimated salvage value in its formula. Therefore, in the final year of the asset's life, the asset must only be depreciated to a net book value equal to its expected salvage value.

**Red Flags.** The basis for long-lived asset valuation is historical cost. Because depreciation does not measure actual decline in value, the net book value of a long-lived asset (historical cost-accumulated depreciation) is not a good measure of the cost of replacing the asset. Neither is net book value a good measure of what the asset would bring if sold. Long-lived assets with net book value equal to their estimated salvage value—or zero if there is no salvage value—may continue to be used by the company to earn revenue while they are minimally valued on the balance sheet.

Depreciation computations are based largely on estimates of both useful life and salvage value. Should either of these estimates change during the life of the depreciable asset, the company will recompute depreciation from that point forward. This computation will use the net book value as the historical cost and the new estimates of salvage and remaining years of useful life. For example, suppose that management decides at the beginning of the third year that an asset that cost $10,000 and had a $1000 salvage value and a three-year estimated useful life now has a remaining useful life of three years with a new estimated salvage value of $1500. Straight-line depreciation expense for that third year would be computed as follows: $10,000 – $6000 = $4,000, the net book value after two years of straight-line depreciation, then ($4000 – $1500)/3 years remaining life = $833 depreciation expense per year.

Comparability is hindered by using different depreciation methods. In our examples, the first year's depreciation expense was: straight-line—$3000, units of production—$2250, sum-of-the-years' digits—$4500, and double-declining balance—$6667. If four identical companies each used a different one of these depreciation methods to compute depreciation for an identical asset, their net book values of the asset and their net incomes would be different. In other words, choice of depreciation methods can create artificial differences between companies.

# 23

# INTANGIBLES AND OTHER ASSETS

Intangible assets are long-lived productive assets that do not have a physical existence. For the most part, they are legal rights given to the company that offer it a competitive edge and aid it in producing revenue. Examples of intangible assets include patents, copyrights, trademarks and tradenames, franchises, organization costs, and purchased goodwill.

Initially, intangible assets are recorded at historical cost. As this historical cost is written off against production periods (see Key 24), the recorded value of the intangible will decline. As with inventories and property, plant and equipment, intangible assets are carried on the balance sheet at the lower of their net historical cost or market value.

There are six major types of intangible assets along with a catchall category, Other Assets.

**Patents.** A patent is an exclusive right to use, manufacture, or sell a product or process. In the United States, patents are granted for 20 years. The patent's historical cost will be expensed against the revenues it helps produce over the lesser of its legal life or its estimated economic life. In fields where technology is rapidly changing (such as computer hardware and software) a patent's economic life may be less than its legal life.

**Copyrights.** A copyright gives exclusive control to the creator of a literary, musical, or artistic work. Copyrights may be assigned or sold. Currently, copyrights are granted for the life of the creator plus 70 years. However, a copyright's historical cost will be expensed over the lesser of its estimated economic life or legal life. The historical costs of literary and musical copyrights are frequently expensed over the life of the first printing.

**Trademarks and Tradenames.** These symbols or words serve to identify a product or company. They are initially granted for 20 years and are subject to indefinite renewals. Theoretically, then, they have unlimited lives and therefore, they are not amortized. They will be reported on the balance sheet at the lower of either their historical cost or their market value.

**Franchises.** A *franchise* is the right to sell a product or service under a tradename. The cost of the franchise will be expensed over the life of the franchise.

**Purchased Goodwill.** When one business purchases another, it may be willing to pay more for that business than the market value of the net assets. (Net assets represent the difference between the value of a company's total assets and its total liabilities.) To an accountant this "excess of cost over the market value" is goodwill. Why might a company be willing to pay more than market value for the net assets of another company? The reason is generally that the purchaser is also acquiring intangibles—the reputation of the products or service of the purchased company, its personnel's potential, monopoly position, etc.

Accounting principles allow only purchased goodwill to be recorded in the accounts (internal development of a business reputation may not be assigned a value and recorded). Goodwill has an indefinite economic life. Therefore, it is not amortized and is reported in the balance sheet at the lower of either its historical cost or its market value.

**Research and Development Costs.** These are the costs of discovering new technology and applying it to products, process, or services. Occasionally, research and development costs will be recorded as assets and amortized over their economic life. However, accounting principles require that the majority of research and development costs be expensed as they arise. This is owing to the uncertainty of future benefits. In fact, most research and development projects do not result in a marketable product, process, or service.

The total cost of research and development for the fiscal period must be disclosed. While the majority of projects may not succeed, they keep a company competitive. The proportion of dollars spent on R & D to a company's sales is one measure of management's investment in the future.

**Other Assets.** This catchall category includes business resources that cannot be classified as current assets, investments, property, plant, equipment, or intangibles. It may include long-lived assets awaiting sale and no longer being used in production. Classifying such assets under Property, Plant and Equipment would imply they are currently in use. Prepayments of expenses (such as a three-year insurance policy) may also be classified as "other." A note on intangible assets is shown below.

Note 15: *Intangible assets are recorded at cost less amortization. Goodwill has indefinite life and is recorded at the lower of cost or market.*

|  | Estimated Remaining Life* | 2009 | 2008 |
|---|---|---|---|
| Patents | 6 | $1,057 | $1,234 |
| Goodwill |  | 639 | 639 |
| Other intangible assets | 25 | 257 | 257 |
| Total |  | $1,953 | $2,144 |

*Weighted average, in years, at December 31, 2009.

# 24

## DEPLETION AND AMORTIZATION

The key to understanding *depletion* and *amortization* is to understand how accountants use the terms. Depletion and amortization (like depreciation) represent the assignment of historical cost of a long-lived asset to production periods—the matching of the costs of production (expenses) with production's results (revenues). This cost assignment is called *depletion* for natural resources and *amortization* for intangible assets.

The method of depletion most often used is a units-of-production formula:

Cost of the natural resource /
estimated recoverable (removable) units of the resource
= per-unit depletion rate

If a stand of timber cost us $2 million and we estimate that it will produce 4 million cords, our depletion rate is $.50 per cord ($2 million/4 million). If we remove 500,000 cords in one year, our depletion expense for that year would be 500,000 × $.50) = $250,000.

Amortization is usually recorded on a straight-line basis (cost / number of amortization periods). The amortization period is the lesser of the intangible's economic life or legal life. Suppose we develop a patented process to use in the production of our product. The research and development costs were $15 million and were expensed throughout the research and development phase (see Key 23). Attorneys' fees and patent application costs totaled $500,000 (the amount recorded as the historical cost of the patent). We estimate that the patented process will have an economic life of 12 years, so we will expense this patent over the 12-year period rather than its legal life of 20 years. Amortization expense will be ($500,000/12) = $41,667 per year.

Amortization is also taken on "Leasehold Improvements" and "Property Subject to Capital Leases" (see Key 21). If leased property will be returned to the lessor at the end of the lease term, the recorded cost of improvements to the leased property will be expensed over the term of the lease. If the company will keep the property after the expiration of the lease, it should expense the improvements and property over their economic lives. In this case, the method of computing amortization should be the method we use to depreciate similar assets that we own.

**Red Flags.** Just as is the case with depreciation, the net book values of natural resources and intangibles are not good measures of either the cost of replacing these assets or the amount that could be received if they were sold. Depletion and amortization computations are based only on estimates, which are of course subject to change. When an estimate changes, the net book value of the asset at that time becomes the basis for depletion or amortization over the remaining units of the natural resource or amortization period.

# 25

# INVESTMENTS

A company may invest its idle funds many ways. For example, it could choose to leave them in a savings account, put them in certificates of deposit, or invest them in stocks or bonds of other companies. This chapter will discuss how a company reports its investments in stocks and bonds in the balance sheet.

Short-term investments (expected to be held for less than one year) are current assets. Long-term investments are generally reported in their own section of the balance sheet between Current Assets and Property, Plant and Equipment.

Just as with other assets, there are different methods for reporting the value of an investment in the balance sheet: (1) market, (2) present value (discounted net cash flows), and (3) the equity method. The classification of an investment and how it is valued and accounted for is determined by marketability, management's intent, and the investment's type. Securities for which an established, ready market exists are said to be marketable. Generally, this includes all securities traded on an exchange or in over-the-counter markets. Closely-held securities are characterized as not marketable only because they are not widely or frequently traded through organized markets.

Five classifications of securities are used to express management's intent: (1) trading securities, (2) securities available for sale, (3) securities held-to-maturity, (4) securities held to obtain significant influence, and (5) securities held to obtain controlling interest.

**Trading Securities** are those stocks and bonds management purchases with the intent of selling them in the near future. They are short-term investments of idle cash

71

which will be sold as management needs money for operations. Trading securities are classified as current assets. Trading securities are reported in the balance sheet at market value.

**Securities available for sale** are those stocks and bonds management intends to hold indefinitely. Common stock is included in this category only when the company owns <20% of the outstanding shares. Securities available for sale are current assets if management believes they may be tempted to sell them within the upcoming year. Otherwise, securities available for sale are presented on the balance sheet as long-term investments. Securities available for sale are reported in the balance sheet at market value.

**Securities held-to-maturity** are those investments in bonds that management intends to hold until they are redeemed by the issuer. These investments are presented on the balance sheet as long-term investments. Bonds that management intends to hold-to-maturity are reported in the balance sheet at present value.

**Securities held to obtain significant influence.** When investors can exercise significant influence over the affairs of the company in which they have invested, the equity method of accounting is used. Investors gain significant influence by buying common stock and holding it as a long-term investment. If an investor owns, say 20% or more of a corporation's outstanding common stock, the investor may be able to elect 20% of the directors. Accountants assume that significant influence exists once an investor acquires 20% or more of a company's common stock.

**Securities held to obtain controlling interest.** If an investor owns >50% of outstanding common shares of a company, the investor has effective control of that company through the ability to elect the majority of the directors. This is termed a parent-subsidiary relationship and accounting rules require a consolidated financial statements presentation (see Key 48).

**Market Accounting Method.** When an accountant uses the market method, the investments are recorded on the balance sheet at their current market value. Securities that are considered not marketable are valued at their acquisition costs. Using the market method, income from the investment is recorded when dividends are declared or interest is earned.

Suppose we invest in a single share of two stocks, UVW, Inc., and XYZ, Ltd. The cost of UVW is $100, and we pay $200 for XYZ. At the end of the fiscal year UVW is selling for $110 per share. XYZ is selling for $160 per share. We would combine these stocks in a portfolio (trading securities or securities available for sale), and then compare the beginning-of-the-year market value of this portfolio to its current market value. In our case, the market value of our portfolio at the beginning of the year (cost) is $300 ($100 + $200). Our stock's current market value is $270. Because the current market value of our portfolio is $30 less than its original cost ($300 – $270), we write it down in value at $30 and report it on the balance sheet at $270. The write-down is called an unrealized loss.

If the investments are trading securities, the unrealized loss is recorded in the income statement as expense or loss. Trading securities are held as part of routine operations—investments of idle cash until the cash is needed for operations. Their change in value is part of current operating income.

If the investments are securities available for sale, the unrealized loss reduces the investment portfolio to its current market value and reduces owners' equity by deducting from owners' equity the unrealized loss of $30. These investments are not considered "cash" available for operations, so their change in value is not part of current operating income, rather it is an adjustment to owners' equity.

When we prepare the next balance sheet, if the stocks' market values are $350, we will write them up in value at $80 ($350 – $270). If the investments are trading securities, we will record the difference on the income statement as revenue or gain. If the investments are securities available for sale, we will increase the investment account to $350 and increase owners' equity $80. This is done by removing the negative owners' equity account Unrealized Loss of $30, and replacing it with additional owners' equity, Net Unrealized Gain of $50. Note the current market value is $50 above the original investment price.

**Equity Accounting Method.** An accountant using the equity method initially records the investment at historical cost. As the company (the investee) earns income, the investors record their share as income from investment. This will increase the value of their investment. But as dividends are paid to them, they reduce the value of their investment because dividends are assumed to be a return of prior earnings, a withdrawal of investment. Recording income and dividends in this manner causes the investment account to mirror the changes that are occurring in the investee's owner's equity.

For example, assume that we buy 10,000 of the outstanding shares of CDE Corporation for $2 million. This investment represents one third of the outstanding shares. CDE's owners' equity has a recorded value of $6 million. Our investment account will reflect one third of CDE's owners' equity, or:

Investment  $ 2,000,000  |  CDE's Owners' Equity    $ 6,000,000

If CDE has net income of $900,000 for the year, our investment will increase $300,000, or:

| Initial Investment | $ 2,000,000 | CDE's Owners' Equity | $ 6,000,000 |
|---|---|---|---|
| + Income | 300,000 | + Income | 900,000 |
| | $ 2,300,000 | | $ 6,900,000 |

Next, CDE pays $450,000 in dividends; we receive $150,000. The dividends are a withdrawal of investment and will reduce our investment account, or:

| Initial | | | |
|---|---|---|---|
| Investment | $2,000,000 | CDE's Owners' Equity | $ 6,000,000 |
| + Income | 300,000 | + Income | 900,000 |
| – Dividends | (150,000) | – Dividends | (450,000) |
| | $2,150,000 | | $ 6,450,000 |

Notice that each time CDE's equity increases or decreases, our investment increases or decreases proportionately. Because we own one third of CDE, our investment is recorded at one third of the value of CDE's owners' equity. If we had paid more than $2 million for our investment in CDE, the excess amount paid would be considered goodwill (see Key 23). Accounting rules require that goodwill be carried at lower of, cost or market value. If the market value of the goodwill declines, the investor will write down the investment, recognizing a loss.

**Present Value.** Long-term investments in bonds expected to be held-to-maturity are recorded at present value. The present value of a bond is its cash value at a point in time. Suppose we can buy a ten-year, $1000 bond that pays 10% interest annually for $950. We will record our investment at $950. If we hold the bond until it matures we will receive a total of $1050 more than we originally invested. Each year, for ten years, we will receive $100 of interest income. The additional $50 (the discount) is earned by holding the bond. (We will receive $1000 at maturity, but we only invested $950.) Each year we record part of the $50 as being earned. One way to record this is to assume that the discount is earned equally during the holding period (straight-line amortization). In this case we would earn in $5 of the discount each year. Each year as we record the discount as being earned, the investment will be increased in value $5 and interest income will be reported as $105 ($100 plus $5 of discount earned). By maturity the investment must have a recorded value of $1000. That is its cash value at that point in time.

**Red Flags.** There are many ways to value investments. Be sure you understand how an investment has been valued and classified. The potential exists for making a company appear more liquid (see Key 54) by manipulating balance sheet presentation. Securities available for sale may be classified as either current or noncurrent assets.

Classification is based on management's ideas about when they will sell a particular security. If management believes they need to appear more liquid by showing more current assets relative to current liabilities, they may shift more of these securities to current assets.

In addition to the general rules we have given you here, special industries have their own valuation methods. For instance, investment companies and brokerage firms value all of their investments in stocks and bonds at current market value, recording all value changes as part of current operating income.

# 26

# CURRENT LIABILITIES

Current liabilities are those obligations of the business that are expected to be paid within one year of the date on the balance sheet. These liabilities include:

**Trade Accounts Payable.** Amounts owed to suppliers for merchandise or services. For example, an unpaid invoice for merchandise purchases, or the utility bill.

**Short-term Notes Payable.** Short-term interest bearing debt. Notes are formal documents showing the amount borrowed (principal) and stating as an annual rate the percentage interest that must be paid. Only the principal is recorded on the balance sheet under the title "Notes Payable." Any interest that the company owes is called interest payable.

**Current Portion of Long-term Debt.** The portion of principal on long-term debt that will be paid within the year. Long-term debt is usually payable in installments (for example, mortgage payments). Any unpaid interest on long-term debt is recorded as interest payable.

**Interest Payable.** The unpaid interest on short-term and long-term debt. This is the interest charge for the days from the last payments to the balance sheet date.

**Unearned Revenues.** When customers pay for products or services in advance, a liability is created. Revenue will not be recorded until the product is delivered to the customer or the service is completed. (See a discussion of revenue recognition in Key 6.)

**Tax and Other Withholdings.** Employers are required to withhold income taxes and Social Security

77

taxes (FICA taxes) from employees' paychecks. These withholdings plus additional FICA taxes and unemployment taxes must be paid quarterly.

**Income Taxes Payable.** The portion of income taxes the business has not yet paid. These are taxes due on the company's earnings (not withholdings as above).

**Contingencies.** A number of "likely to occur" contingencies are recorded as liabilities (see Key 9). Examples are, "Vacation Wages Payable" and "Estimated Liabilities Under Warranties." "Vacation Wages Payable" is not paid until the employees have taken their vacations. "Estimated Liabilities Under Warranties" is the estimated cost of repairing any defective items manufactured and sold under warranty. Only the portion of the contingencies expected to be paid in the coming year is classified under current liabilities. Be sure to read the notes to the financial statements to get a feel for how significant the contingencies are.

A note relating to current liabilities reported in the balance sheet is shown below.

10. Current liabilities (in thousands)

|  | 2009 | 2008 |
|---|---|---|
| Trade accounts payable | $ 30,520 | $ 39,022 |
| Other accounts payable | 8,011 | 9,382 |
|  | $ 38,531 | $ 48,404 |
| Insurance | $ 14,611 | $ 14,616 |
| Interest | 8,934 | 7,352 |
| Pensions | 7,358 | 9,925 |
| Payroll and vacation pay | 7,338 | 9,920 |
| Taxes other than income taxes | 2,268 | 4,653 |
| Other | 21,692 | 15,914 |
|  | $ 100,732 | $ 110,784 |

# 27
# NONCURRENT LIABILITIES

Noncurrent (or long-term) liabilities are those obligations of the business that are not expected to be paid for at least one year from the date on the balance sheet. Noncurrent liabilities are carried at their present values. This is the amount of money the company could pay to settle the debt at the balance sheet date. It excludes any future interest, which is not yet due. Most noncurrent liabilities call for periodic payments of principal and interest. The portion of principal that will be due within the year will be classified as a current liability (see Key 26).

Examples of noncurrent liabilities include Long-term Notes and Mortgages Payable, Bonds Payable (see Key 28), Obligations Under Capital Leases (see Key 9), Unfunded Accrued Pension Cost (see Key 10), and Deferred Tax Liability (see Key 43).

Unless you carefully read the notes to the financial statements you will not understand noncurrent liabilities. Many long-term debt covenants place restrictions on the borrower. For instance, a debt covenant may require us to maintain a 2:1 current ratio (the ratio of current assets to current liabilities—see Key 54). What if our current ratio is only 1.9:1? Then we are technically in default on our long-term obligation and it can be called due at any time. Unless management believes the deficiency can be corrected within the specified grace period, the debt will have to be reclassified as current.

**Settling Debt Before Maturity.** Sometimes a company will pay off debt before it is due. Any settlement of debt before its due date will cause the company to report a gain or loss. The company will have a gain if the cost of settling the debt is less than the debt's recorded value on the balance sheet (including any interest due). The company will have a loss if the cost of settling the debt is greater than the debt's recorded value on the balance sheet (including any interest due). Why might a company take a loss to settle a debt before it is due? The loss may be less than the future interest payments, or the company may now be able to borrow money at lower interest rates.

**Troubled Debt Restructurings.** Sometimes a company experiences problems repaying its debts. A troubled debt restructuring is a situation in which the creditor grants concessions to help the debtor avoid defaulting. The concessions may take the form of the debtor's transferring assets or stock to the creditor, or modifying the terms of debt.

The creditor may agree to settle the debt for noncash assets or stock with a market value less than the recorded value of the debt (including any interest due). In this case the debtor will report a gain on the restructuring equal to the amount by which the debt exceeds the market value of the assets given the creditor. The gain will generally be reported on the debtor's income statement as an extraordinary item.

When the creditor agrees to modify the terms of debt (principal, interest rate, length of time, etc.), the debtor may have to pay more or less than the recorded value of the debt plus any interest due. If the total of the new payments called for is less than the recorded value of the debt (including any interest due), the debtor will record a gain—again, generally reported as an extraordinary item. Payments made by debtors after restructuring are considered to be payments of principal.

These debtors will not recognize interest expense; they could not even pay the debt owed, let alone additional interest.

On the other hand, what if modifying the terms of debt results in total payments that exceed the recorded value of the debt (including any interest due)? In this case the debtor will recognize the recorded value of the debt as the principal of the restructured debt. The amount by which the new payments exceed this principal is the debtor's interest expense over the remaining term of the debt.

A typical schedule of long-term debt, showing interest rates and repayment dates, follows.

## Long-term Debt

| (In thousands) | January 30, 2009 | February 1, 2008 |
|---|---|---|
| Industrial revenue bonds, net of expenses (a) | $ 74,174 | $ 80,763 |
| Mortgage notes payable at annual interest rates from 7⅛% to 11% (b) | 13,708 | 14,013 |
| Japanese yen loan payable at 5.15%, due 2007 | 13,644 | — |
| Japanese yen loan payable at 6.46%, due 2012 | 80,260 | — |
| British pound sterling 11% Stepped Coupon Guaranteed Bonds, due 2017 | 193,180 | — |
| 8¼% sinking fund debentures, due 2017, net of discounts | 88,013 | 87,910 |
| 8¼% debentures, due 2021, net of expenses | 197,906 | 197,832 |
| | 660,885 | 380,518 |
| Less current portion | 397 | 638 |
| | $660,488 | $379,880 |

(a) Bank letters of credit of $57,135,000, expiring in 2010, support certain industrial revenue bonds. The Company expects the bank letters of credit expiring in 2010 will be renewed. The bonds have fixed or variable interest rates with an average of 3.2% at January 30, 2009.
(b) Mortgage notes payable are collateralized by property and equipment with an aggregate carrying value of $19,278,000 at January 30, 2009.

The fair market value of the Company's long-term debt at January 30, 2009 is approximately $728,000,000. The fair market value was estimated using quoted market rates for publicly traded debt and estimated current interest rates for nonpublic debt.

81

The annual maturities of long-term debt at January 30, 2009 are as follows:

| Year ending in | (In thousands) |
| --- | --- |
| 2010 | $ 397 |
| 2011 | 405 |
| 2012 | 1,519 |
| 2013 | 1,531 |
| 2014 | 1,477 |
| 2015 and subsequent | 655,556 |
| | $ 660,885 |

**Red Flags.** There is generally no problem understanding the noncurrent liabilities section of the balance sheet, other than the areas cited above (early extinguishment, troubled debt restructuring). Most difficulties arise in interpreting bonds payable, discussed in the next Key. The appropriateness of a company's debt level can be evaluated by comparing a ratio of debt to total assets to the standard industry ratio.

# 28

# BONDS AND AMORTIZATION

When a company needs to borrow a large amount of money—perhaps $20 million—it has two basic choices: It can seek one lender who will supply the entire $20 million or it can seek a series of smaller lenders and obtain the total amount needed in several smaller sums. A company that issues bonds is taking the second option. A typical corporate bond is a debt agreement for $1000. Thus, a $20 million debt is divided into 20,000 bonds, each for a debt of $1000.

When an investor (lender) "buys" $50,000 in bonds, the investor has, in essence, agreed to lend the company $50,000. The interest rate, interest payment schedule (usually semiannual), and bond maturity date (when the principal amount is returned) are all contained in the bond. The bond debt may be secured (backed by collateral) or unsecured. Bonds for unsecured debt are called *debentures*. All the bonds may be retired (repaid) at the same time, or they may be structured to mature (come due) in increments. Bonds that mature in increments are called *serial bonds*.

**Amortization.** A typical bond might be for a debt of $1000 for ten years, with interest at 10% per year, paid semiannually. The company is, in essence, making two promises: (1) to pay the lender $1000 in ten years, and (2) to pay interest of $100 (1000 × .10) each year. As long as the market rate of interest is 10% for bonds of that particular type (secured or unsecured), for the same term and for companies in the same risk class, the company can issue the bond without problem, receiving $1000.

83

But, suppose the interest rate rises before the bond is issued. A lender would then no longer purchase a $1000 bond (and agree to lend $1000) for 10% interest. The lender would either demand a higher current yield or would insist on investing less than $1000 in order to receive the payments (principal and interest) described in the bond agreement. Perhaps the lender would agree to lend only $900 in exchange for the payments described in the bond. But the bond issuer would still pay:

| | |
|---|---:|
| 1. At the end of ten years | $1,000 |
| 2. In equal semiannual payments each year ($100 × 10) | $1,000 |
| Total amount paid | $2,000 |
| Less amount received from lender | 900 |
| Excess paid over amount received | $1,100 |

The excess paid over the amount received is the *true cost* of the funds. The company pays $100 cash in interest per year, but the true average annual cost of the money borrowed is $110 (1100/10) per year. The company records the $100 cash outflow each year and the $110 average annual expense. The extra $10 is the amortization of the excess paid over the amount received. (The amortization of bond investments is explained in Key 25.)

When bonds are presented in an annual report, details of the security agreement (if any), the maturity dates, and the interest rates will be in the notes to the financial statements. The bonds are shown under long-term debt in the liabilities section of the financial statements. When a bond is issued at face (for $1000), the bond will be presented in the balance sheet as follows:

Bond payable (see note x)          $1,000

If the market interest rate is more or less than the interest in the bond agreement, the bonds will be sold at a discount or premium, and presentation will be different. If a bond was issued for $900 (as described above), it would appear in the financial statements as follows:

Bond payable (see note x)          $1,000
less discount on bonds payable          100          900

Bonds sold for more than face amount are presented in a similar fashion. A bond issued for $1100 would appear in the financial statements with a premium rather than a discount.

Bonds payable (see note x)          $1,000
plus premium on bonds payable          100          1,100

A schedule of bonds payable (debentures), disclosing the interest rates and maturity dates, is shown below.

**Long-term Debt**

| December 31, | 2009 | 2008 |
|---|---|---|
| Sinking fund debentures: | | |
| 8⅛% due 2015–2020 | $ 100,000 | $ 100,000 |
| 10% due 2016–2021 | 100,000 | 100,000 |
| 9¼% due 2019–2030 | 125,000 | 125,000 |
| Debentures 9½% due 2015 | 100,000 | 100,000 |
| Debentures 9¼% due 2020 | 125,000 | 125,000 |
| Debentures 8½% due 2027 | 100,000 | 100,000 |
| Notes 7⅜% due 2014 | 50,000 | 50,000 |
| Medium-term notes due 2012–2015; 6% to 9½%; weighted average rate 9% | 230,000 | 270,000 |
| Lease obligations under Industrial Revenue Bonds; due 2012–2014; 4% to 8%; weighted average rate 6¼% | 68,287 | 62,705 |
| Notes payable to Industrial Development Authorities; due 2011–2024; 3¼% to 8%; weighted average rate 6½% | 232,395 | 232,530 |
| Other notes due 2010–2016 | 14,225 | 24,471 |
| Total | $ 1,244,907 | $ 1,289,706 |

# 29

# OWNERS' EQUITY

*Equity* is simply a term meaning "property rights." When the balance sheet components were discussed in Key 17, it was evident that the total assets, or properties, owned by the company belonged to one of two parties—the creditors of the company or its owners. The equity (property rights) of creditors is called debt or liabilities. The equity (property rights) of owners is called owners' equity, stockholders' equity, or (sometimes) capital. The amount of owners' equity can be calculated by subtracting the creditors' equity (liabilities) from the total assets of the company, as: $A - L = OE$. Expressed in this form, owners' equity is sometimes called "net assets," meaning "assets net of (less) liabilities."

The key to understanding owners' equity is to realize that both amounts—liabilities and owners' equity—represent claims of parties against the assets (again, property rights), but the amounts also represent the sources of the assets.

When creditors have transactions with a company, the transactions are commonly described as being "at arm's length." But when owners have transactions with their own company, it is as related parties, not at arm's length. Since owners can legally remove capital as dividends only under certain conditions and only from certain sources, the focus in accounting for owners' equity is on sources of capital.

A complex owners' equity presentation could have capital that came from many sources:

Donations (see Key 33)
Treasury stock transactions (see Key 31)

Preferred stock (see Key 30)
Subscribed stock (see Key 33)
Common stock (see Key 30)
Appropriated retained earnings (see Key 32)
Unappropriated retained earnings (see Key 32)

A simple owners' equity section from an actual balance sheet is shown below.

| **Stockholders' Equity** (in thousands) | 2008 | 2007 |
|---|---|---|
| Preferred stock—cumulative— | | |
| $1.00 par | | |
|   Authorized—10,000,000 shares | | |
|   Issued and outstanding—none | | |
| Common stock—$1.00 par value | | |
|   Authorized—100,000,000 shares | | |
|   Issued—22,048,624 shares in 2008 | | |
|   and 16,252,655 shares in 2007 | 22,049 | 16,253 |
| Additional paid-in capital | 154,850 | 59,667 |
| Retained earnings | 60,554 | 45,848 |
| Foreign currency translation | | |
|   adjustment | 938 | — |
| | 238,391 | 121,768 |
| Less 50,289 shares in 2008 and | | |
| 21,764 shares in 2007 of | | |
|   common stock in treasury—at cost | 687 | 274 |
| | 237,704 | 121,494 |

For each issue of stock, the number of shares authorized, issued and outstanding and the par or stated value is given. Dividend and call values are included for preferred stocks. The nature of any appropriation of retained earnings is disclosed. Some information about owners' equity will be included in the body of the financial statements. Additional information will be disclosed in the notes.

# 30

# CLASSES OF STOCK

Basically, all stock issued by a company is either preferred stock or common stock, regardless of what name the stock may be given. And, although some companies may describe several different types or classes, there is (except in very rare cases) only one class of common stock. All other classes of stock, regardless of name, are preferred in some way over the one class of common stock.

If a company is liquidated, all creditors are paid proceeds of the liquidation before the claims of stockholders are considered. Among the different classes of stock, there is a ranking as to preference in receiving the proceeds of the liquidation. The stock with the lowest preference as to assets on liquidation is common stock. All other classes of stock are classes of preferred stock, since those stockholders have preference over common stockholders in liquidation and, as will be discussed, perhaps in other ways as well.

By virtue of their bottom ranking as to claims on assets on liquidation, common stockholders are said to be the residual equity holders; they receive any residue left after all creditors and all holders of other classes of stock have been paid. Common stockholders may receive nothing, or they may receive a great deal when a company is liquidated. All creditors and preferred shareholders have a contractually stated amount that they will receive if the company is liquidated and funds are available. Common stockholders have no such contractually stated amount. Thus, common shareholders take the greatest risk but may also receive the greatest reward.

Dividends on preferred stock usually must be paid before dividends on common stock are paid. If the company does not create enough earnings so that the board of directors can declare dividends for both common and preferred shareholders, common shareholders may receive no dividends.

On the other hand, preferred shareholders have no voice in company management. They are, in fact, more like long-term bondholders (creditors) than owners: both receive a fixed payment each year (as dividend or interest), and both have preference over common stockholders as to assets on liquidation, but neither has a vote in company management. The difference is that unless the company has insufficient assets, long-term bondholders will eventually be repaid their investment, and preferred stockholders will not.

To understand preferred stock, there are three additional points we must address.

1. *Dividend calculation.* The dividend rate for preferred stock is a set amount each year. The dividend is usually stated as a dollar amount per share (i.e., a $5 preferred share pays $5 dividends) or as a percentage of par value (i.e., an 8%, $100 par-value preferred share pays $8 dividends). Par value is an arbitrary amount assigned to shares of stock, both common and preferred. *Par value* (and a similar term, *stated value*) had meaning decades ago when securities regulations were different, but have little significance now, other than as a vehicle for calculating dividends on preferred stock or, occasionally, a discount on common stock.

2. *Obligation for missed dividend payments.* If the dividend agreement on preferred stock is *cumulative*, a company must catch up any missed dividend payments to preferred shareholders before dividends can be paid to common shareholders. This is important. A company has no legal obligation to pay dividends until they are declared by the board of directors. Thus, even though preferred dividends are set, there is no guarantee that they will be paid until they are declared by the board. For example, assume dividends to preferred shareholders would total $100,000 per year, but the company does not

declare and does not pay dividends for years 1 and 2. In year 3, the board declares total dividends of $350,000. If preferred dividend payments are cumulative, the distribution schedule is shown below.

For Preferred Stock:

| | |
|---|---:|
| Current year dividend (Year 3) | $100,000 |
| Prior year dividends (Years 1 and 2) | 200,000 |
| Total dividends for preferred stockholders | $300,000 |
| Available for dividends to common stockholders | 50,000 |
| Total dividends paid | $350,000 |

A noncumulative distribution of the same $350,000 under the conditions described is shown below.

For Preferred Stock:

| | |
|---|---:|
| Current year dividend (Year 3) | $100,000 |
| Prior year dividend (Years 1 and 2) | 0 |
| Total dividends for preferred stockholders | $100,000 |
| Available for dividends to common stockholders | 250,000 |
| Total dividends paid | $350,000 |

3. *Conversion privilege.* Some preferred stock agreements contain an option allowing the preferred stock to be exchanged for a set number of common shares. To make preferred shares more attractive to investors, the stock may be convertible to common shares in some ratio (10 shares of common for 1 share of preferred, for example).

A financial statement excerpt showing common and preferred stock is presented below.

## Stockholders' Equity

|  | 2008 |
| --- | --- |
|  | (in thousands) |
| Preferred stock, authorized 25,000,000 shares; outstanding 2,875,000 Series C $2.875 cumulative convertible, par value $1.00 per share, (liquidation preference $143,750,000) | $ 2,875 |
| Common stock, par value $1.00 per share, authorized 150,000,000 shares; outstanding 53,444,467 at March 31, 2008 | 53,444 |
| Capital in excess of par value | 730,987 |

Publicly traded companies with mandatorily redeemable preferred stock—stock redeemable by the holder for a stated price at a certain point in time—are required to report that stock as a liabililty. Accountants believe this type of stock possesses more of the characteristics of debt than ownership. Mandatorily redeemable stock carries a fixed redemption price, and usually cumulative dividends. Cumulative dividends guarantee the holder a return, if not through quarterly dividend payments, then by overtaking the dividend payments at the point of redemption. Thus, mandatorily redeemable preferred stock appears to possess debt characteristics similar to those of a zero-coupon bond, a bond for which no interest is paid until maturity.

Presented below is a partial balance sheet showing the placement of mandatorily redeemable preferred stock followed by the accompanying note.

| At December 31, (Dollars in millions, except per share amounts) | 2009 | 2008 |
|---|---|---|
| Long-term debt | $ 17,646.4 | $ 13,265.2 |
| Employee benefit obligations | 10,384.2 | 10,004.4 |
| Deferred credits and other liabilities | | |
| Deferrred income taxes | 2,253.8 | 2,106.2 |
| Other | 550.9 | 772.6 |
| | 2804.7 | 2878.8 |
| Preferred stock of subsidiary | 145.0 | 145.0 |
| Shareowners' investment | | |
| Series preferred stock ($.10 par value; none issued) | — | — |
| Common stock ($.10 par value; 1,576,246,325 shares and 1,576,052,790 shares issued) | 157.6 | 157.6 |
| Contributed capital | 13,368.0 | 13,176.8 |

Our subsidiary Bonhe has the authority to issue 5,000,000 shares of Serial Preferred Stock. Bonhe has issued two series of preferred stock.

In 2000, Bohne issued 850,000 shares of Series A Preferred Stock at $100 per share with an annual dividend rate ot $7.08 per share. In 2002, 600,000 shares of Series B Preferred Stock were issued at $100 per share with an annual dividend rate of $5.80 per share. Both series are subject to mandatory redemption on May 1, 2012 at a redemption price per share of $100, together with any accrued and unpaid dividends.

# 31

# TREASURY STOCK

Stock issued by a company may later be reacquired by the company. In some cases, the company may retire or cancel this stock. When reacquired stock is not retired or canceled, it is referred to as treasury stock.

Treasury stock is not an asset. A company cannot create an asset by holding stock in itself. Although treasury stock, like retired stock, represents a decrease in outstanding stock, the reduction in shares outstanding is not made on the balance sheet. The treasury stock is shown as a reduction in stockholders' equity in one of two ways.

1. The treasury stock may be shown at par value as reduction in common stock.

### Stockholders' Equity

| | | |
|---|---|---|
| Contributed capital: | | |
| Common stock at par | $500,000 | |
| Less treasury stock at par | 100,000 | |
| | $400,000 | |
| Paid in capital in excess of par | 80,000 | $480,000 |
| Retained earnings | | 200,000 |
| Total stockholders' equity | | $680,000 |

2. The treasury stock may be shown at reacquisition cost as a reduction of total stockholders' equity.

### Stockholders' Equity

| | | |
|---|---|---|
| Contributed capital: | | |
| Common stock at par | $500,000 | |
| Paid in capital in excess of par | 80,000 | $580,000 |
| Retained earnings | | 200,000 |
| Total | | 780,000 |
| Less treasury stock at par | | 100,000 |
| Total stockholders' equity | | $680,000 |

Under either method, total stockholders' equity is decreased by the purchase of treasury shares.

Just as treasury stock is not an asset, a loss or gain cannot result from treasury stock transactions. "Things" happen that you and I would call a "loss" (reacquiring treasury stock for $20 per share and later reissuing it for $12) or a "gain" (reacquiring treasury stock for $30 per share and later reissuing it for $40). But it is illegal for a company to produce a gain or loss by transacting in its own stock. When total stockholders' equity is decreased by treasury stock transactions (a loss), the decrease is generally taken directly from retained earnings. No loss is recorded.

When total stockholders' equity is increased by treasury stock transactions (a gain), the increase is recorded as a separate source of capital called Paid-in Capital from Treasury Stock Transactions.

# 32

# RETAINED EARNINGS AND APPROPRIATIONS

When we discussed owner's equity in Key 29, we pointed out that the components of owners' equity represented both property rights and sources of assets. Retained earnings is the dollar amount of assets furnished by earnings of the company that were not distributed as dividends. The key to understanding retained earnings is to realize that such earnings do not represent cash but are only a source of assets.

This logic can be expanded. If a company earns $500,000 and does not declare dividends, retained earnings would be increased by the $500,000 retained in the business. But what does a company do with this $500,000? Management may expand the business (buy new equipment or increase inventories, for instance) or may repay an outstanding loan. The $500,000 increase in retained earnings documents a source of net assets (assets minus liabilities), but does not indicate which assets were provided by the income.

In addition to being a source of assets, total retained earnings is also the maximum amount that can be distributed to stockholders as dividends. The company probably does not have cash available to pay dividends in the amount of retained earnings (nor would the company wish to, if earnings can be reinvested in the business). A company frequently distributes a portion of each year's earnings as dividends in some general pattern, perhaps some amount per share or some percentage of earnings. The remainder is reinvested in the business.

A company that embarks on a special project may limit dividend payments until the project is completed. The company may be required to do this by a major creditor or may simply limit dividend payments in order to preserve cash for expansion. When management limits dividend payments, there are two methods of notifying stockholders: (1) explain the action in the notes to the financial statements, or (2) appropriate a portion of retained earnings.

The portion of retained earnings listed as appropriated in the owners' equity section of the balance sheet is not available for dividend payments. When the project is completed, appropriated retained earnings are unappropriated and again available for dividend payments. Cash may have been spent on the project (building a plant, retiring bonds) and the composition of assets changed, but retained earnings are unaffected except for changing the designation of the appropriated component back to unappropriated. A note discussing appropriated and unappropriated retained earnings is shown below.

7. Retained Earnings.

The provisions of certain of the Company's loan agreements limit the payment of cash dividends under certain circumstances. Retained earnings not restricted under these provisions at December 31, 2007, 2006, and 2005 were $231 million, $202 million and $266 million, respectively.

**Red Flags.** Companies may use an appropriation of retained earnings simply to reduce the size of unappropriated retained earnings "available" for dividends. Uninformed investors may believe they should receive more of the earnings retained in the business, or labor unions may believe that wages should be higher—neither group realizing that the retained earnings are invested in equipment, in building new plants, or in acquiring more inventory, thus creating the potential for more profit for owners and wages for workers.

# 33

# DONATED CAPITAL AND SUBSCRIBED STOCK

When companies issue stock, they may do so outright, selling stock and receiving cash, property, or services in exchange—or stock may be issued on a subscription basis. A stock subscription is a legally binding contract between the issuing company and the subscriber or purchaser of the stock. Stock subscription agreements allow payment for the stock to be deferred. In these cases, the company has a legal claim for the contract price of the stock, and the purchaser has the legal status of a stockholder (unless specific rights are withheld by state law or contract).

The company's legal claim to the stock contract price is recorded in the balance sheet as "Stock Subscriptions Receivable." Stock subscriptions are like other company receivables: the purchaser/stockholder pays against the outstanding balance according to the contract agreement. But they are different from other receivables in that they are not current assets. Stock subscriptions receivable are subtracted from the common stock accounts to show that the stock is not fully paid for. The stock certificates are ordinarily not issued until the contract price is paid in full.

When the subscription agreement is signed, the subscribed common stock is shown in the owners' equity section of the balance sheet as an increase in two accounts:

1. The par value of the stock is recorded in an account called "Common Stock Subscribed."

2. Any excess over par value is recorded in the account "Premium on Common Stock" or "Paid in Capital in Excess of Par."

When the subscribed stock is fully paid, there will be no subscription receivable carried in current assets and "Common Stock Subscribed" is transferred to "Common Stock."

When property or services are donated to a company, the value of the asset is included in income as a gain. This reflects the idea that all increases in the value of assets, other than through borrowing or additional investments by owners, are income.

**Red Flags.** While a stock subscription agreement is a legal contract and the subscription receivable is a legitimate receivable, corporate policy and state law vary as to how a defaulted subscription is treated. When a subscriber defaults, the company may take any of the following actions:

1. Refund amount received.
2. Refund amount received less cost of reselling the stock.
3. Declare amount received as forfeited by the subscriber.
4. Issue shares equal to the amount already received.

# 34

# STOCK ISSUED TO EMPLOYEES

Many companies allow employees to purchase ownership shares. If shares are available to all employees who meet limited employment requirements, such as a minimum tenure with the company and the employee purchase price is 95 percent or more of the market value at the time the shares are purchased, accounting rules will not consider the discount part of employee compensation and their value will not be included as additional wage or compensation expense in the computation of net income (see Key 40). On the other hand, many companies have stock incentive plans for top management. If certain performance targets are met for the year, top management can receive stock, stock options, or stock appreciation rights. Because these benefits are not available to all employees, they are considered compensation for management services to the company and will require recognition of additional wage or compensation expense.

**Stock Options** are instruments that give the holder the right to acquire ownership shares at a set price (option price). If the company's stock is selling for more in the open market than the option price (the price to the holder of the option), the options will usually be exercised. Options generally have an expiration date beyond which they may not be exercised (tendered with cash for stock).

**Stock Appreciation Rights** are instruments that give the holder the right to take appreciation beyond some base value in either cash or stock of the company. The base for an appreciation right is generally the current market value of the stock at the time the right is issued to the employee. Thus, if the stock rises in value the employee can take the gain in value in either cash or stock. Appreciation rights also have an expiration date beyond which the employee loses the right to take the gain in value in cash or stock.

**Accounting for Options and Appreciation Rights.** As stated above, if the options or appreciation rights are not considered compensation to the employee for services rendered, no value is placed on these options or rights, and expense is not recorded. For options that are considered compensation, the company must record compensation expense using the fair value method.

**Fair Value Method.** Under this method, the compensation cost recorded by the company is the market value of the options to purchase shares. The fair value method requires that this measured compensation cost be matched to the year in which the employee provides the services for the options or shares. For example, suppose that an employee is granted options to receive 100 shares of stock after 2 years of service. At the time the plan is announced, these options could be sold in the market for $30 each ($3,000 total). The compensation expense that the company must record is a total of $3,000 over the 2-year period, or $1,500 per year. After the employee has worked 2 years, the options may be converted to stock if the employee wishes.

Sometimes, in addition to surrendering the option, an employee will also have to pay some cash to obtain the shares. This cash amount is known as the option price and affects only the value at which the stock is recorded on the issuing company's books. It does not affect the valuing of, or recording of, compensation expense. The total value assigned to the stockholder's equity when an option is exercised is the market value of the option when the plan was authorized plus the option price. Suppose in the previous example the option price is $15 per share. When the option is converted to stock, the employee must surrender the option, which was valued at $30, and $15 cash. The total value recorded in stock-holder's equity for the new share issued is $45.

Recognition of compensation cost for appreciation rights differ in that they have a base value and any change in value over time is recorded as either an increase or decrease in compensation expense. Thus, if an employee receives appreciation rights when the market value of the company's stock is $30 per share and at the end of the fiscal year the stock sells for $37 per share, the company will recognize $7 per right as compensation expense. If at the following year-end, the market value dropped to $36 per share, the company will record a $1 per right decrease in compensation expense. This adjustment continues until the rights are exercised at which time the exact amount of compensation is locked down.

**Restricted and Pseudo Stock.** Many companies' stock award plans will limit employees to owning restricted or pseudo shares. Restricted shares are actual shares of stock that may not be resold to anyone other than the employee's company. Generally, upon termination of employment the employee must resell his shares to the company. Because these shares are actual shares that without restriction could have been traded in the open market, the market value of the same type of stock is used in computing the fair value of the options, rights, or shares. Pseudo shares are shares that the company is not authorized to issue to anyone other than employees. Since they are not publicly traded, they have no established market value. Their market value is estimated with reference to the market value of the company's actual trading stock using techniques developed by financial analysts. This estimated value then becomes the "market value" when computing the fair value of the options, rights, or shares issued to employees.

The following note describes one company's accounting for employee stock plans.

**Restricted Stock Plans.** Under the Company's restricted stock plans, common stock may be awarded to key employees, officers, and nonemployee directors. The recipient is entitled to all the rights of a shareholder, except that during the forfeiture period, the shares are nontransferable. The awards vest over a specified time period but typically either immediately vest or cliff vest over a three-year period with service as the vesting condition. Upon issuance of stock under the plan, fair value is measured by the grant date price of the Company's shares. This fair value is then expensed over the restricted period with a corresponding increase to additional paid-in capital. A summary of nonvested restricted shares at October 31, 2008, and changes during the year ended October 31, 2008, is presented below:

|  | Shares | Weighted-Average Grant Date Fair Value Per Share |
|---|---|---|
| Nonvested at October 31, 2007 | 115,650 | $ 22.31 |
| Granted | 33,885 | 40.50 |
| Vested | (6,750) | 17.60 |
| Foreited | (18,000) | 20.87 |
| Nonvested at October 31, 2008 | 124,785 | $ 27.71 |

The weighted-average grant date fair value of restricted stock granted during the years ended October 31, 2008, 2007, and 2006 was $40.50, $27.33, and $18.70, respectively. The total fair value of restricted stock vested during the years ended October 31, 2008, 2007, and 2006 was $0.1 million, $0.4 million and $0.3 million, respectively. Total unrecognized compensation cost related to unamortized restricted stock awards was $1.3 million as of October 31, 2008. That cost is expected to be recognized over a weighted-average period of 1.4 years.

**Red Flags.** Over the years, additional stock compensation of management became as important as the salary paid, and it is often valued at more than the manager's cash salary. Some authorities assert that this can lead to a conflict of interest. Unscrupulous managers may take action based on what will maximize their personal chance at stock bonuses regardless of whether that action is good for the company. Read the notes carefully to determine the fair value of the options, rights, or stock issued to executives. The fair values assigned to options and stock issued to employees are expensed as the employee earns those options or shares, and are reported in stockholders' equity as shares issued or pending issue. The fair value assigned to appreciation rights is expensed as the employee earns those rights, and usually appears as a liability in the balance sheet because the employee generally has the right to take the increase in value in cash at his or her option.

# 35

# INCOME STATEMENT COMPONENTS

Annual business income or loss is computed by subtracting the expenses that occurred during the year from the revenues earned during the year. If revenues exceed expenses, the business has earned income. If expenses exceed revenues, a loss has occurred. Revenues and expenses are recorded at the time they are earned or occur regardless of when cash is received or paid. This is the accrual concept, which is used to measure business activity and income (see Key 46).

The income statement reports the results of business activities for a period of time (typically a fiscal year). These results are classified as revenues and expenses. Revenues measure the inflow of new assets to the business; expenses measure the outflow of assets or the using up of assets in that same process. Net income represents an increase in assets and owners' equity, while a net loss represents a decrease in assets and owners' equity.

A classified income statement contains the following sections:

| | |
|---|---|
| Sales or Operating Revenues: | Net sales revenues (sales less returns) or service revenues are reported in this section (Key 36). |
| *minus* | |
| Cost of Goods Sold: | The amount the company paid for the inventory it sold. A service organization will not have this expense. |
| *equals* | |

| | |
|---|---|
| Gross Profit on Sales: | The difference between net sales revenues and the cost of goods sold. From this profit margin, the company must cover all other costs if it expects to have net income. A service organization will not report a "gross profit on sales." |
| *minus* | |
| Operating Expenses: | Selling and general and administrative expenses (Key 40). Service organizations will not divide their expenses between selling and general and administrative categories. |
| *plus* | |
| Other Revenues (Gains): | Increases in asset value from transactions not directly related to operations. For instance, interest earned on investments arises from a decision related to managing idle cash. That decision is not related to trying to earn a profit through sales or by providing services. |
| *minus* | |
| Other Expenses (Losses): | Decreases in asset value occur from transactions not directly related to operations. For instance, interest expense arises from the decision to finance operations by increasing debt. That decision is not related to trying to earn a profit through sales or by providing services. |
| *equals* | |
| Pretax Income from Continuing Operations: | The sum of all the revenues and expenses related to the portion of the business that is continuing. |
| *minus* | |
| Income Tax Expense: | A function of pretax income from continuing operations and the appropriate tax rates (see Key 43). |
| *equals* | |

105

Income from       After-tax income of the portion of the
Continuing        business that is continuing.
Operations:
      *plus or minus*
Discontinued      Either an after-tax gain or loss on a seg-
Operations:       ment of the business that management
                  intends to sell (see Key 41).
      *equals*
Income Before     A subtotal.
Extraordinary
Items:
      *plus or minus*
Extraordinary     After-tax gains or losses on unusual
Items:            transactions (those not expected to
                  recur) (see Key 42).
      *equals*
Net Income        The total of all reported revenues (gains)
(loss):           and expenses (losses).

Earnings Per      Publicly traded companies are required to
Common Share:     present several ratios that summarize
                  the assumed income earned by each
                  holder of a share of common share.
                  Earnings-per-share ratios are the com-
                  pany's income divided by an average
                  number of common shares assumed to
                  be outstanding (see also Key 50).

## An example of a classified income statement:

**Consolidated Statements of Earnings**

| in thousands, except per share amounts | Year Ended November 30 | | |
|---|---|---|---|
| | **2009** | **2008** | **2007** |
| Net Sales | $598,149 | $297,405 | $267,321 |
| Cost of goods sold | 381,013 | 202,836 | 182,247 |
| Gross profit | 217,136 | 94,569 | 85,074 |
| Selling, general and administrative expenses | 152,076 | 69,383 | 65,521 |
| Interest expense | 15,426 | 1,860 | 2,458 |
| Earnings from continuing operations before income taxes | 49,634 | 23,326 | 17,095 |
| Income taxes | 26,263 | 11,698 | 8,579 |
| Earnings from continuing operations | 23,371 | 11,698 | 8,516 |
| Loss from discontinued operations | — | — | (3,651) |
| Earnings before extraordinary item | 23,371 | 11,628 | 4,865 |
| Extraordinary item— termination of defined benefit pension plans, less applicable income taxes of $1,599 | — | — | 1,877 |
| Net Earnings | $ 23,371 | $ 11,628 | $ 6,742 |
| Earnings per common share Basic | | | |
| Earnings from continuing operations | $ 1.15 | $ .72 | $ .53 |
| Loss from discontinued operations | — | — | (.23) |
| Extraordinary item | — | — | .12 |
| | $ 1.15 | $ .72 | $ .42 |
| Diluted | $ 1.12 | | |
| Average number of common shares outstanding | | | |
| Basic | 20,293 | 16,225 | 16,201 |
| Diluted | 22,615 | — | — |

**Red Flags.** Not all income statements will include every section presented above. For instance, in a year in which a company does not have discontinued operations or extraordinary items, those sections will drop out of the income statement. Care should be taken when comparing income statements over time. Income from continuing operations is comparable to a later year's net income taken from an income statement that does not have discontinued operations, extraordinary items, or a change in accounting principle.

# 36

# SALES AND OTHER REVENUES

Revenues (the money the company receives for its merchandise or services) are generally recorded at the time of sale or completion of the service. However, two conditions must be met before revenue can be recorded. First, the earnings process must be substantially complete, and, second, collectibility of the revenue can be estimated. The earnings process is not substantially complete if:

1. The seller and buyer have not agreed on the price of the merchandise or service
2. The buyer does not have to pay the seller until he resells the merchandise
3. The buyer does not have to pay the seller if the merchandise is stolen or physically destroyed
4. The buyer and seller are related parties (for example, parent and subsidiary)
5. The seller must still provide significant services to the buyer or aid in reselling the product

If substantial performance has occurred and the collectibility of the revenue can be estimated, the sale of the product or service can be recorded. (Key 37 discusses estimating the collectibility of credit sales and accounting for bad debts.) If a company cannot estimate the collectibility of a sale, it will record the revenue only as the customer makes payments. This has the effect of recording the sale on the basis of when the cash is received rather than when it is earned (the accrual basis—see Key

46). Accountants use either the installment method or the cost-recovery method to record revenue as the customer makes payments.

The installment method records part of each payment as revenue. Suppose we sold merchandise that cost us $4000 for $10,000. The gross profit on the sale is $6000 ($10,000–$4000) or 60% of the sales price ($6000/$10,000). As the customer makes payments, $60 of each $100 collected will be reported as revenue. The revenue that has not yet been collected will be recorded as "Deferred Gross Profit" in the liability section of the balance sheet.

The cost-recovery method does not record revenue until the customer has paid the seller for his cost of the merchandise sold. Using the example given above, we would have to receive $4000 from the customer before any revenue would be recorded. After we recover the cost of the merchandise ($4000), each dollar received is recorded as revenue.

If a company provides services on a long-term contract, revenue may be recorded over the life of the contract. The construction industry records revenue on major long-term contracts as the work is performed rather than at the point of sale. If dependable estimates of selling price, construction costs, and stage of completion exist, the construction company will record revenue as the work is performed. Accountants call this the percentage-of-completion method.

For instance, suppose we are involved in a three-year construction project. The first year we estimate that we are one third complete. The second year we are two thirds complete.

Then we finish the project on schedule in the third year. We will record one third of the estimated gross profit (sales price less the total estimated construction cost) as revenue in the first year, another one third of the estimated gross profit in the second year (2/3 – 1/3 reported the first year), and the final one third as revenue in the third year.

While the percentage-of-completion method departs from the concept of recording revenue at the point of sale, it is consistent with the accrual concept of measuring activities in the period in which they occur. If a company does not have dependable estimates of the sales price, construction costs, or stage of completion, it will not recognize revenue until the project is complete (year 3 in our example).

A note to the financial statements showing the revenue components for a business segment is shown below.

Supplemental gaming segment operating data for the three years ended December 31, 2009 are as follows:

| (In thousands) | | 2009 | 2008 | 2007 |
|---|---|---|---|---|
| Revenue | | | | |
| Rooms | $ | 120,948 | 104,348 | 90,785 |
| Food and Beverage | | 109,933 | 92,822 | 87,728 |
| Casino | | 265,313 | 219,138 | 204,649 |
| Promotional allowances | | (34,921) | (27,891) | (26,637) |
| Other products and services | | 27,346 | 19,534 | 10,127 |
| Total | | 488,619 | 407,951 | 366,652 |

Segmented reporting is discussed in more detail in Key 11.

# 37

# BAD DEBTS

When a company accounts for bad debts, both the income statement and the balance sheet are affected. The estimate of bad debts is shown in the income statement. The estimate of uncollectible accounts is shown as a subtraction from total accounts receivable in the current assets section of the balance sheet (see Keys 18 and 19).

The key to understanding the accounting treatment of bad debts is to realize that the amounts involved are estimates of amounts that may be uncollectible. There are two goals in accounting for bad debts. One is to match the cost of bad debts to the sales revenue produced in the period. This means that, of necessity, some estimation must take place. At the end of the year, some credit sales will have resulted in accounts receivable that have already proven to be uncollectible. Other uncollected sales will not yet be known to be bad debts. An estimate of the uncollectible amount must be made if the company is to charge this year's profits with the bad-debts expense that result from this year's sales. If the company waits until each account proves to be uncollectible (or collectible), the costs of bad debts in one year may not be recognized until the next year. Bad-debts expense must be matched to the year benefited by the original sale. (The accounting concept of matching is explained in Key 6.)

The second goal in accounting for bad debts is to place a correct valuation on the amount of accounts receivable shown in the current assets section of the balance sheet. These accounts are all open; the company has not yet decided that any of them is definitely a bad debt. (When an account is judged to be uncollectible, it is removed from the accounts receivable.) As a result, the allowance for bad debts shown as a deduction from accounts receivable in the balance sheet is wholly an estimate. A note describing a reserve for bad debts is shown below.

*Reserve for credit losses*
The reserve for credit losses is established to absorb future losses from the credit portfolio based on management's judgment. Factors considered in determining the level of the reserve include industry concentrations, specific known risks, adequacy of collateral, past experience, the status and amount of nonaccrual, past due and restructured loans, off-balance sheet credit risks, and current as well as anticipated economic and political conditions that may affect certain borrowers. Credit losses are charged against the reserve; recoveries are added to the reserve.

**Red Flags.** There is some conflict between the two goals in accounting for bad debts—maximizing the accuracy of the income statement versus maximizing the accuracy of the balance sheet. Estimates of bad debts will occasionally be high or low, particularly on interim (quarterly) statements, but rarely on annual reports. To prevent misstatement, a company that does not relate the amount of bad debts expensed to sales activity will be required periodically to examine the outstanding accounts receivable in detail and justify the estimates that appear in the financial statements.

# 38

# COST OF GOODS SOLD AND INVENTORIES

Inventories were discussed in Key 20 as a component of the current assets section of the balance sheet. This key will help you understand the relationship between cost of goods sold in the income statement and the balance in inventory on hand in the balance sheet.

The total inventory available for sale each year is the total of the beginning inventory and the inventory purchased during the year. At year end, typically, part of the total inventory available for sale during the year is still on hand and part of it has been sold. The total cost of inventory available for sale is thus split between ending inventory in the balance sheet and the cost of goods sold in the income statement.

At first glance this may seem to be no problem. Indeed, if all units were purchased at the same price all year, there would be no problem. The problem is that most companies purchase units at many different prices, and, depending on the method used to flow costs through inventory, ending inventory and cost of goods sold can be any one of several different figures—all of which are acceptable for financial reporting!

The key to understanding inventory and cost of goods sold is to realize that when units are identical, accountants are free to flow costs through the accounting records in ways that do not mimic the way the actual goods are handled.

To illustrate, assume that a company has no beginning inventory and purchases three *identical* units during the first quarter of the year: one in January, one in February, and one in March. The units are purchased for $4, $6, and $8 each. Now assume that one unit is sold for $10. What would the gross profit be?

If the company charges the $4 cost of the first unit purchased to cost of goods sold, gross profit would be $6 and ending inventory could be $14 ($6 + $8) for the two units still on hand. If the company charges the $6 cost of the second unit purchased to cost of goods sold, gross profit will be $4 and ending inventory will be $12 ($4 + $8). Finally, if the last unit purchased is expensed first, gross profit and ending inventory will be $2 and $10, respectively. These three alternatives are shown below.

|  | Alt. 1 | Alt. 2 | Alt. 3 |
|---|---|---|---|
| *In the income statement:* | | | |
| Selling price | 10 | 10 | 10 |
| Cost of goods sold | 4 | 6 | 8 |
| Gross Profit | 6 | 4 | 2 |
| *In the balance sheet:* | | | |
| Ending inventory | 14 | 12 | 10 |
|  | (6+8) | (4+8) | (4+6) |

The first possibility above would result if a company uses a FIFO (first-in, first-out) inventory flow. With FIFO, accountants flow costs the way merchants typically flow goods: the oldest units are sold first. The most recently purchased units are in ending inventory.

The third possibility results when a company uses the LIFO (last-in, first-out) method of inventory flow. Using LIFO, the cost of the most recent purchases are charged to cost of goods sold and the old costs remain in inventory, regardless of how the company flows the physical units.

The key to understanding the accounting logic behind LIFO inventory is to think about the result of the sale. How much better off is the company after selling one unit for $10? Is it $6 better off? Or $4? Or $2? To answer this question, we must think carefully. If the company is to remain in business, management must replace any units sold. How much will the next unit cost? The last purchase was for $8 per unit. Prices are rising ($4 to $6 to $8 per unit). The next, reasonably, will be for $8 per unit or more. If the company must replace the unit sold, the company is only $2 better off ($10 – $8 = $2), having sold one unit for $10. The logic that supports LIFO, flowing costs in a LIFO pattern regardless of the flow pattern of physical units, would increase the accuracy of the income statement.

The last possibility is a compromise between flowing costs as merchants flow inventory and maximizing the accuracy of the income statement. This method, called the Weighted Average Method, charges both ending inventory and cost of goods sold with the weighted average cost of all units available for sale. The weighted average cost per unit is $4 + $6 + $8 equals $18 divided by three units equals $6 per unit, as above.

**Red Flags.** The financial statement reader must realize that the use of different inventory methods results in financial statements that are not comparable. The inventories, cost of goods sold, and profit measures (gross profit and net income) of a company that uses LIFO cannot be compared to the same measures from a company that uses any other inventory method.

Many companies that use LIFO report lower earnings than companies using FIFO or weighted average. The LIFO company may, however, pay less tax (on the lower earnings) and, as a result, have much better cash flows than companies using other inventory methods. It is much better, all else being equal, to report lower earnings and pay less tax. LIFO gives a firm lower earnings and a tax advantage during inflationary periods when prices are rising.

# 39

# MANUFACTURING COSTS

Manufacturing costs are considered assets and are part of the cost of manufactured units in inventory until the units are sold. When an assembly line worker or factory foreman is paid, the wages are charged, not to a wage expense account, but directly, or through overhead, to an inventory of unfinished work in process (an asset). When prepaid insurance on the factory expires month by month, it is charged, not to insurance expense, but through overhead to an inventory of unfinished work in process (an asset).

There are three categories of manufacturing costs—labor, materials, and overhead—and they are all charged to the asset called work-in-process inventory. When financial statements are prepared, work-in-process inventory is shown in the current assets section of the balance sheet or is disclosed in the notes to the financial statements.

Manufacturing costs differ from nonmanufacturing costs in the timing of their charge against earnings. Nonmanufacturing costs, such as selling or administrative costs, are called *period costs* because they generally become expenses over a period of time. When a sales salary is paid, for example, it is immediately charged to sales salaries expense because the benefit of the salary was consumed in the period during which the salesperson made sales calls. When a year's insurance is paid on the corporate office building, however, the insurance cost is expensed month by month, as time passes, and the insurance (with its benefit as an asset) expires.

When units are completed, all the manufacturing costs charged to work-in-process inventory are transferred to finished-goods inventory, another asset account. Only when the finished goods are finally sold are the manufacturing costs transferred to an expense account, cost of goods sold. Because manufacturing costs are not expensed until the product is sold, manufacturing costs are called *product costs*.

The flow of manufacturing costs is illustrated below:

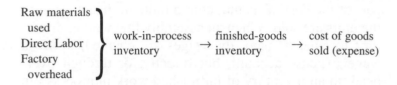

Raw materials used
Direct Labor
Factory overhead
} work-in-process inventory → finished-goods inventory → cost of goods sold (expense)

Factory overhead is the conglomeration of all the indirect costs of production, that is, all manufacturing costs except raw materials and labor used directly in the product. Factory overhead includes the costs of supervisory personnel, maintenance, factory and equipment depreciation, general supplies, energy, insurance, and any other manufacturing cost associated only indirectly with individual units produced.

**Red Flags.** The accounting method that charges all manufacturing costs to units produced is called *full* or *absorption costing*. Because absorption costing charges fixed capacity costs (such as supervision and factory depreciation) to individual units produced, net income is biased optimistically (high) when inventories are increasing, and pessimistically (low) when inventories are decreasing. The full explanation of why this happens is very complex, but the net effect is that in times of growth, when inventories are increasing, actual profits may not be quite as great as reported, and in times of recession, when inventories are shrinking, profits may not be as low as financial statements indicate.

# 40

# OPERATING EXPENSES

In a financial statement, expenses (the costs of producing sales of products or services) are matched against the revenues they produce (see the discussion of matching in Key 6). Costs directly associated with producing a certain revenue are expensed in the same period that the revenue is recorded. The costs of long-lived assets, on the other hand, are expensed over the assets' expected lives (see Key 22). Other costs that benefit only the current period are expensed as they arise.

In a business that sells merchandise, the major operating expense is the cost of merchandise sold (see Key 38). This cost is recorded on the income statement below net sales. The difference between net sales and cost of goods sold is gross profit on sales, the profit margin that must cover all other costs if the company expects to have net income.

Other operating expenses are reported on the income statement after gross profit on sales (see Key 35). These operating expenses may be divided into selling and administrative expenses. *Selling expenses* are the costs associated with producing sales, and *administrative expenses* are the costs associated with managing the company.

The expenses listed are only representative of the types of costs that will be classified as selling or administrative expenses. In fact, few companies disclose the breakdown of their operating expenses. When a company does provide breakdowns, the actual costs and breakdowns may vary depending on the nature of the business. For instance, a service-oriented business may not break out its expenses into selling and administrative categories.

A schedule of operating expenses extracted from an income statement is shown below.

|  | 2009 | 2008 | 2007 |
|---|---|---|---|
| Salaries | $ 508 | $ 480 | $ 393 |
| Employee benefits | 78 | 99 | 117 |
| Net occupancy expense | 167 | 123 | 110 |
| Equipment expense | 93 | 91 | 68 |
| Net expense of real estate acquired | 94 | 12 | 6 |
| Amortization of goodwill and other intangibles | 43 | 27 | 16 |
| Forms and supplies | 34 | 32 | 29 |
| Shares, capital and franchise taxes | 22 | 18 | 14 |
| Other expense | 364 | 263 | 213 |
| Total operating expense | $ 1,403 | $ 1,145 | $ 966 |

# 41

# DISCONTINUED OPERATIONS

The decision to discontinue a business operation creates a contingency, which we defined in Key 9 as a situation in which the company stands to gain or lose as the result of a past transaction or event. Only the amount of gain or loss is "contingent"—that is, dependent on another transaction or event. Whenever management decides to sell a segment of the business (the event giving rise to future gain or loss), a contingency is created. At that point, management may not know whether the sale will result in a gain or loss. Even if management has a buyer, the exact gain or loss may not be known until the disposal date.

Although these gains and losses are contingent, disclosure of discontinued operations differs from the guidelines for disclosure of "likely" contingencies. These gains and losses are reported in the income statement in the period in which they occur.

Gains or losses on discontinued operations are reported in a special section of the income statement. That section follows income from continuing operations and precedes extraordinary items (see Key 35). Discontinued operations will be reported net of (including) their tax effects. Gains generally give rise to additional taxes, while losses generally result in tax savings. It is necessary to include all tax consequences in reporting discontinued operations because of the structure of the income statement. Income tax expense has been computed on income from continuing operations. To include in this calculation the one-time tax gain or loss from a sale would distort the income from continuing operations.

In the year in which management decides to sell the segment, two categories of discontinued operations may appear: first, gain or loss from operating the discontinued segment; second, gain or loss on disposal of the segment. Immediately, upon the board of directors voting to sell the segment, it is reclassified as held for sale and the company must compare the accounting book value of the unit to its market value. If the market value is lower, the company will write down the unit's value to market and include the loss, net of its tax effect, in the first figure: gain or loss from operating the discontinued segment. Also included in gain or loss from operating the discontinued segment is the segment's net income or loss from the beginning to the end of the fiscal year or disposal date, whichever comes first. The second figure, gain or loss on disposal of the segment, is the gain or loss on disposal of the assets, net of its tax effect.

Most dispositions will be reported on two income statements. Because disposal of a large business segment is a lengthy process, it is seldom accomplished within one fiscal period. Let's look at a simple example of a disposal.

Whatsit, Inc. decides to sell the Widget division to Wangsung, Ltd. The decision to sell is made at the October 1, 2008 board meeting. On October 1, 2008, the accounting book value of Widget is $500,000,000, while its fair market value is $490,000,000. Thus, Widget's assets are overvalued on the books by $10,000,000. Widget's combined tax rate is 30 percent. Widget also experiences the following gains and losses from the beginning of 2008 until final disposition on May 1, 2009:

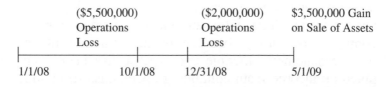

The following partial income statements illustrate Whatsit's presentation of the discontinued operation in its financial statements for 2008 and 2009.

**2008 Income Statement:**

| | |
|---|---:|
| Pretax income from continuing operations | $ 20,000,000 |
| Less: Provision for income taxes | 6,000,000 |
| Income from continuing operations | 14,000,000 |
| | |
| Discontinued Operations: | |
| Loss from operation of Widget division ($5,500,000 + $10,000,000 loss on write down, net of $4,650,000 tax savings) | (10,850,000) |
| Net Income | $ 3,150,000 |

**2009 Income Statement:**

| | | |
|---|---:|---:|
| Pretax income from continuing operations | | $ 24,000,000 |
| Less: Provision for income taxes | | 7,200,000 |
| Income from continuing operations | | 16,800,000 |
| | | |
| Discontinued Operations: | | |
| Loss from operation of Widget division ($2,000,000, net of $600,000 tax savings) | ($1,400,000) | |
| Gain on Sale of Widget division ($3,500,000, net of $1,050,000 taxes) | 2,450,000 | |
| Net Gain from Discontinued Operations | | 1,050,000 |
| | | |
| Net Income | | $ 17,850,000 |

**Red Flags.** Segregating gains or losses on discontinued operations on the income statement alerts the reader of the financial statements to the fact that a significant portion of the business will no longer be contributing to the company's earnings. In this situation, income from continuing operations (rather than net income) becomes the important figure when trying to forecast the future earning ability of the company.

Not all sales of business assets, segments, or divisions will be reported as discontinued operations. Only those operations that can be separated operationally, physically, and from the accounting records are considered segments when reporting discontinued operations. Gains or losses on disposal of business assets that cannot be separated operationally, physically, and from the accounting records will be reported as part of income from continuing operations.

# 42

# EXTRAORDINARY ITEMS

Before a company can classify a gain or loss as an extraordinary item, two criteria must be met: the gain or loss will come from a transaction or event that is (1) unusual, and (2) nonrecurring. An *unusual transaction* or event is one that is unrelated to the typical activities of the business. A *nonrecurring transaction* or event is one that management does not expect to occur again.

The key to understanding extraordinary items is that both criteria must be met before a company can classify a gain or loss as extraordinary. The classification is company-specific. Natural disasters meet the definition of unusual (unrelated to the typical activities of the business). But, for an orange grower in North Florida a freeze would not be considered nonrecurring and could not be considered extraordinary. On the other hand, an earthquake in New York City would give rise to an extraordinary loss. The criteria of "unusual" and "nonrecurring" must be looked at from the perspective of the reporting company. Is the transaction or event unusual given the nature of that company's business and geographical location?

**Presentation of Extraordinary Items.** Extraordinary gains or losses are reported in their own section on the income statement, between discontinued operations and the cumulative effect of a change in accounting principle (see Key 35). A net extraordinary gain (gain less additional income taxes) will increase income, while a net extraordinary loss (loss reduced by income tax savings) will decrease income. Accountants report extraordinary items net of their tax consequences. If a gain (or loss) is extraordinary, then so are the tax liabilities (or benefits) that it generates.

Segregating extraordinary gains or losses on the income statement is important. By classifying a gain or loss as extraordinary, management is saying "this is an unusual gain or loss and we do not expect it to recur." Comparability between fiscal years is gained by segregating extraordinary items. Because extraordinary items are not expected to recur, "Income Before Extraordinary Items" is a comparable figure to "Net Income" in years when there are no extraordinary gains or losses. Companies required to report earnings per share (see Key 50) will report these figures both "Before" and "After" "Extraordinary Items," so that there are easy comparisons for years that did not have extraordinary gains or losses.

The presentation of an extraordinary item is shown below.

|  | 2009 | 2008 | 2007 |
|---|---|---|---|
| Income (loss) before extraordinary items and cumulative effect of change in accounting principle | 232 | 699 | (599) |
| Extraordinary items | — | (473) | 18 |
| Net income | $ 232 | $ 226 | $ (581) |

**Red Flags.** Exceptions to evaluating gains and losses by the extraordinary criteria exist. Accounting principles require that certain types of gains and losses *not* be treated as extraordinary items, while other gains and losses must be treated as extraordinary items. Gains or losses that are not to be treated as extraordinary items include: (1) losses from the write-down or write-off of receivables, inventories, equipment, or intangible assets; (2) gains or losses related to foreign currency exchanges;

(3) gains or losses from the sale of a business segment (see Key 41), (4) gains or losses from the sale or abandonment of property, plant or equipment that has been used in the business; and (5) losses resulting from strikes by employees. These types of gains or losses may not receive extraordinary item treatment regardless of the company's line of business or geographical location.

# 43

# TAXES AND TAX DEFERRALS

The key to understanding tax deferrals is to realize that income tax regulations do not always require a company to use the same accounting method on the tax return that it has used on the income statement. Tax expense is related to the revenues and expenses listed on the income statement. In other words, taxes are recorded on the income statement in the same year that the revenues and expenses giving rise to the taxes are reported. This is the matching concept (see Key 6). However, the taxes currently due are related to the figures on the tax return. Accountants call the difference in these two amounts "deferred taxes."

Suppose a company decides to use a different method of depreciation on the income statement than it uses on the tax return. In such cases, depreciation expense on the income statement and on the tax return will be different at various times in the equipment's useful life. Consider this example:

**Annual Depreciation**

|  | Year 1 | Year 2 | Year 3 | Year 4 | Total |
|---|---|---|---|---|---|
| On Income Statement | $10,000 | $10,000 | $10,000 | $10,000 | $40,000 |
| On Tax Return | $13,332 | $17,780 | $ 5,924 | $ 2,964 | $40,000 |
| Difference* | ($3,332) | ($ 7,780) | $ 4,076 | $ 7,036 | $ -0- |
| Difference in Tax (30% rate) | ($1,000) | ($ 2,334) | $ 1,223 | $ 2,111 | $ -0- |

*A negative difference (in parentheses) means that more depreciation will be recorded on the tax return, decreasing the amount of taxes currently due.

In years 1 and 2, this company will record more depreciation on the tax return than on the income statement ($3332 and $7780 more, respectively). This will cause it to pay less in tax than it is showing as tax expense on its income statement ($1000 and $2334 less, respectively). In effect, by claiming more depreciation on the tax return, the company is postponing taxes in years 1 and 2.

In years 3 and 4, the company will show more depreciation on the income statement than on the tax return ($5924 and $2964 more, respectively). This will cause it to pay more taxes than are showing in tax expense for years 3 and 4 ($1223 and $2111 more, respectively). This is the payment of the postponed taxes from years 1 and 2.

You will notice that there is no difference between the income statement and the tax return in total depreciation taken over the four years. Over that same period tax expense will also equal the amount of taxes due. The difference is simply in the timing of the payments and of the reporting.

In the example above, a liability is created in years 1 and 2 for future taxes. This liability is paid in years 3 and 4. The balance sheet prepared at the end of year 1 will show the $1000 deferred tax liability as noncurrent. Deferred tax amounts are classified, current, or noncurrent, based on the characterization of the temporary difference creating them. In this case the difference is caused by depreciation on noncurrent assets, so the deferred tax is noncurrent. The balance sheet at the end of year 2 will show $3334, ($1000 + $2334) as noncurrent deferred tax liability. At the end of year 3, the balance sheet will show a noncurrent deferred tax liability of $2111 ($3334 − $1223).

Recording revenues and expenses on the income statement and tax return in different periods can also produce a deferred tax asset. Suppose that our fiscal year ends on December 31 and that in December 2008 we collect January 2009 rents. Income tax regulations require that we pay tax on the rents in 2000, the year in which they are collected. Under the accrual concept (see Key 6), the rents are not earned until January 2009 even though they must be reported as revenue on the 2008 tax return. Since the rents are unearned, they will be reported as a current liability on the December 31, 2008 balance sheet. The 2008 tax payment will be more than the expense showing on the income statement. We have paid taxes on revenue we have received but have not yet earned (we still owe the tenants occupancy for January or their money back). This prepayment will be treated as a deferred tax asset.

If the company experiences a change in tax rates from one year to the next, it must revise the recorded amount of the deferred tax liability or deferred tax asset. This adjustment will be made through tax expense. Suppose the income statement shows $10,000 more in revenue than the tax return. At a 30% rate this will create a $3000 deferred tax liability. If the tax rate increases to 40%, this will require the deferred tax liability to be increased by $1000 ($10,000 × 40% − $3000). This adjustment will be made by increasing income tax expense by $1000 when the tax rate changes. Tax rates can change either by legislation or because the company moves into a higher (or lower) tax bracket through changes in earnings.

A company should use timing differences to its advantage. Where income tax regulations allow, it can use methods on the tax return that will minimize the amount of taxes currently due, thus creating a deferred tax liability. The advantage of postponing as long as legally possible the payment of tax is that the company then can use those funds to earn additional profits. A note giving the components of income and taxes and explaining the deferred taxes for the year is shown below.

# INCOME TAXES

The provisions for income taxes computed by applying the U.S. statutory rate to income before taxes as reconciled to the actual provisions were:

| | 2008 Amount | 2008 Percent | 2007 Amount | 2007 Percent | 2006 Amount | 2006 Percent |
|---|---|---|---|---|---|---|
| Income before provision for income taxes | | | | | | |
| United States | $ 615 | 56.8% | $ 283 | 24.1% | $ 363 | 43.7% |
| Foreign | 467 | 43.2 | 891 | 75.9 | 467 | 56.3 |
| | $1,082 | 100.0% | $1,174 | 100.0% | $ 830 | 100.0% |
| Taxes at U.S. statutory rates | $ 368 | 34.0% | $ 399 | 34.0% | $ 282 | 34.0% |
| State taxes, net of federal benefit | 22 | 2.0 | 17 | 1.4 | 15 | 1.8 |
| Difference between U.S. and foreign rates | (31) | (2.8) | (28) | (2.4) | (28) | (3.3) |
| Nondeductible amortization | 44 | 4.0 | 37 | 3.2 | 29 | 3.4 |
| Other, net | (25) | (2.3) | (12) | (1.0) | (3) | (.4) |
| Taxes at effective worldwide tax rates | $ 378 | 34.9% | $ 413 | 35.2% | $ 295 | 35.5% |

Current and deferred tax provisions were:

| | 2008 Current | 2008 Deferred | 2007 Current | 2007 Deferred | 2006 Current | 2006 Deferred |
|---|---|---|---|---|---|---|
| United States | $ 175 | $ (7) | $ 98 | $ 24 | $ 76 | $ 54 |
| Foreign | 159 | 17 | 238 | 27 | 142 | — |
| State | 33 | 1 | 21 | 5 | 11 | 12 |
| | $ 367 | $ 11 | $ 357 | $ 56 | $ 229 | $ 66 |

Following are the components of the deferred tax provisions occurring as a result of transactions being reported in different years for financial and tax reporting:

| | 2008 | 2007 | 2006 |
|---|---|---|---|
| Depreciation | $ 1 | $ 8 | $ 53 |
| Unremitted earnings of foreign subsidiaries | 20 | 14 | 6 |
| Inventory valuation methods | (1) | (4) | (3) |
| Other, net | (9) | 38 | 10 |
| | $ 11 | $ 56 | $ 66 |
| Cash payments for income taxes | $304 | $381 | $169 |

131

# 44

# COMPREHENSIVE INCOME

In 1998, a new financial statement made its appearance. The new statement is called a Statement of Comprehensive Income and it is delivered in several formats.

Comprehensive income is the net change in owners' equity during the year from the company's transactions and events that did not involve the owners. In other words, issuance of stock, repurchase of stock, declaration, and payment of dividends are transactions with the owners and as such are excluded from the calculation of comprehensive income. Comprehensive income includes net income (see Key 35) and adjustments to asset and liabilities values that do not affect the current period's net income. If accounting pronouncements require adjustment of an asset or liability's value and recognition of a holding gain or loss as an equity adjustment, that adjustment is part of other comprehensive income (all value changes recorded during the year from non-owner sources). Examples of these types of adjustments include the adjustment to market value for "available for sale securities" (see Key 25) and certain kinds of derivatives (Key 45), as well as, foreign currency translation adjustment arising from restating financials denominated in foreign currency (see Key 60).

Accounting standards permit the display of comprehensive income as an addendum to the income statement, part of the statement of stockholders' equity, or in a separate statement in its own right. An example of the stockholders' equity format appears below.

## Consolidated Statements of Shareowners' Equity

| Three-Year Period Ending December 31, 2009 | Number of Common Shares Outstanding | Common Stock | Paid in Capital | Retained Earnings | Outstanding Restricted Stock | Accumulated Other Comprehensive Income | Treasury Stock | Total |
|---|---|---|---|---|---|---|---|---|
| (In millions except per share data) | — | — | — | 3,492 | — | — | — | 3,492 |
| **Balance December 31, 2008** | 2,505 | $856 | $ 863 | $12,882 | $(68) | $(365) | $(8,799) | $ 5,369 |
| **Comprehensive income:** | | | | | | | | |
| Net income | — | — | — | 3,492 | — | — | — | 3,492 |
| Translation adjustments | — | — | — | — | — | (238) | — | (238) |
| Net change in unrealized gain on securities | — | — | — | — | — | 74 | — | 74 |
| Minimum pension liability | — | — | — | — | — | (8) | — | (8) |
| **Comprehensive income** | | | | | | | | 3,320 |
| Stock issued to employees exercising stock options | 9 | 2 | 122 | — | — | — | — | 124 |
| Tax benefit from employees' stock option and restricted stock plans | — | — | 63 | — | — | — | — | 63 |
| Stock issued under restricted stock plans, less amortization of $15 | — | — | 10 | — | 7 | — | — | 17 |
| Purchases of stock for treasury | (33) | — | — | — | — | — | (1,521) | (1,521) |
| Dividends (per share—$.50) | — | — | — | (1,247) | — | — | — | (1,247) |
| **Balance December 31, 2009** | 2,481 | 858 | 1,058 | 15,127 | (61) | (537) | (10,320) | 6,125 |

The key to understanding comprehensive income is to remember that it includes all value changes recorded during the year from transactions and events not involving the company's owners. Net income is therefore an intrinsic part of comprehensive income, as well as, the adjustments noted above. Regardless of the presentation adopted by the company, all comprehensive income formats contain the same basic information.

# 45

# DERIVATIVES

Derivative financial instruments are financial assets or liabilities whose value is derived from the value of another financial asset. An option is a derivative financial instrument because the value of the options are based on the value of the underlying asset. For example, the value of an option to purchase or sell British pounds depends on the value of the British pound. A derivative instrument is often standardized and traded in secondary markets, or custom-tailored as a contract between two parties. Derivative financial instruments cover a wide variety of financial assets and liabilities used mostly in banking, such as forwards, futures, and option contracts; swaps; swaptions; and hybrid securities including convertible bonds and other debt contracts with equity or income participation. Full definitions and descriptions of all types of derivatives is beyond the scope of this (and probably any other) book.

Accounting valuation rules require companies to report derivatives in the balance sheet at fair market value. The change in value of derivatives entered into to offset the effects of planned transactions is deferred (holding gain or loss equity adjustment) until the related transaction is completed. If everything goes as planned, the value change in the derivative offsets any loss accompanying the transaction. These types of transactions are termed "hedges."

For example, suppose we import cars from Japan and are obligated to repay in Japanese yen (yen-based account payable). The risk we bear is that exchange rates may move against us. The value of the yen relative to the dollar may rise before we are required to repay, thus causing us to pay more than anticipated. To offset this risk, we can purchase a forward or futures contract in yen. These types of contracts lock down the price for yen at today's rate. If the value of the yen relative to the dollar rises we can sell our forward or futures contract (which increased in value) at a gain that should approximate our loss from the rise in the yen value of our account payable.

The change in value of derivatives that are not part of a hedged transaction is reported as a gain or loss in the current period's income statement.

Derivatives are valued by the same methods used for other financial instruments. But, because there is no market or market price for many derivatives, theoretical option pricing models are often used. These methods are complex and hard to understand. In many cases where companies experienced derivative losses, managers who made key decisions admitted they did not fully understand how the derivatives worked or how they were valued.

In addition to being hard to value and understand, derivatives are risky because they represent a zero-sum game. Unlike most business activities where both parties to a transaction benefit (a buyer and a seller both gain from a transaction, for example), when someone benefits from derivatives, someone else loses the same amount. The result is a Las Vegas-style redistribution of wealth, and many companies have gone home losers.

Presented below is an example of one company's note on financial derivatives.

**Derivative financial instruments.** The company utilizes derivative financial instruments to reduce financial market risks. These instruments are used to hedge foreign currency, interest rate and certain equity market exposures of underlying assets, liabilities and other obligations. The company also uses derivatives to create synthetic instruments, for example, buying and selling put and call options on the same underlying security, to generate money market like returns with a similar level of risk. The company does not use derivative financial instruments for speculative or trading purposes. The company's accounting policies for these instruments are based on whether they meet the company's criteria for designation as hedging transactions. The criteria the company uses for designating an instrument as a hedge include the instrument's effectiveness in risk reduction and one-to-one matching of derivative instruments to underlying transactions. Gains and losses on currency forward contracts, and options that are designated and effective as hedges of anticipated transactions, for which a firm commitment has been attained, are deferred and recognized in income in the same period that the underlying transactions are settled. Gains and losses on currency forward contracts, options, and swaps that are designated and effective as hedges of existing transactions are recognized in income in the same period as losses and gains on the underlying transactions arc recognized and generally offset. Gains and losses on any instruments not meeting the above criteria are recognized in income in the current period. If an underlying hedged transaction is terminated earlier than initially anticipated, the offsetting gain or loss on the related derivative instrument would be recognized in income in the same period. Subsequent gains or losses on the related derivative instrument would be recognized in income in each period until the instrument matures, is terminated or is sold. Income or expense on swaps is accrued as an adjustment to the yield of the related investments or debt they hedge.

**Derivative Financial Instruments and Hedging Activities.** The company uses forward foreign exchange contracts, or derivative contracts, to reduce the exchange rate risk of specific foreign currency transactions. These contracts require the exchange of a foreign currency for U.S. dollars at a fixed rate at a future date. The company's strategies to manage the risks associated with foreign currency transactions and the effect of these strategies on the company's consolidated financial statements are as follows:

**Fair value hedging strategy.** The company enters into forward foreign exchange contracts to hedge certain firm commitments denominated in foreign currencies, primarily the euro. The purpose of the company's foreign currency hedging activities is to protect the company from risk that the eventual dollar-equivalent cash flows from the sale of products to international customers will be adversely affected by changes in the exchange rates.

**Cash flow hedging strategy.** To protect against an increase in cost of forecasted purchases of foreign-sourced component parts payable in euros, the company has a foreign currency cash flow hedging program. The company hedges portions of its forecasted purchases denominated in the euro with forward contracts. When the U.S. dollar weakens against the euro, increased foreign currency payments are offset by gains in the value of the forward contracts. Conversely, when the U.S. dollar strengthens against the euro, reduced foreign currency payments are offset by losses in the value of the forward contracts.

To protect against the reduction in value of certain forecasted foreign currency cash flows associated with export sales from October to November 2006 denominated in British Sterling and to protect against increases in the cost of purchases of certain components from October through December 2006 that are payable in euros, each in connection with the company's contract to provide certain wheeled tanker systems to the U.K. MoD, the company has instituted a foreign currency cash flow hedging program. The company hedges portions of its estimated foreign currency cash flows in connection with the U.K. MoD contract.

**Deferred hedging gains and losses.** At September 30, 2006, the U.S. dollar equivalent of outstanding forward foreign exchange contracts totaled $49,872 in notional amounts, including $28,661 in contracts to sell British Sterling, $6,018 in contracts to purchase British Sterling, $14,189 in contracts to purchase euros, and $1,004 in contracts to sell euros. At September 30, 2006, net unrealized losses (net of related tax effect of $3,336) related to foreign exchange forward contracts totaling $5,680 have been included in accumulated other comprehensive income (loss). During fiscal 2007 all pretax losses on derivative instruments are expected to be reclassified out of accumulated other comprehensive income (loss) into earnings, as amounts being hedged are reflected in earnings.

Net gains or losses related to hedge ineffectiveness included in income were insignificant for all years presented.

**Red Flags.** Derivatives are not fully understood nor are the methods of estimating their value simple. For example, one implementation guide *"explaining"* the rules on derivatives runs 576 pages long. While estimates of fair value and inclusion of financial derivatives in companies' balance sheets as assets and liabilities is better than not disclosing these risks, estimates are just that—best guesses!

# 46

# ACCRUAL ACCOUNTING VERSUS CASH FLOW

The *accrual principle* attempts to translate into dollars of profit or loss the actual activities of the fiscal period. The accrual principle is a combination of two ideas, revenue recognition and matching.

The *revenue recognition principle* provides that revenue (sales price) be recorded when the necessary activities to sell a good or provide a service have been completed. Revenue is recorded at the time of sale regardless of whether cash is collected or a receivable from the customer is created at that time.

The *matching principle* tells the accountant when to record a production cost as an expense. Costs directly associated with producing a certain revenue will be expensed in the same period that the revenue is recorded. But the cost of long-lived assets will be expensed over their expected lives, and other costs that benefit only the current period are expensed as they arise.

Under the matching principle an expense can be recorded before, after, or at the time a cost is actually paid. From the accountant's point of view it is the earnings activity that gives rise to the conversion of cost to expense—it does not matter whether that cost has been paid or a liability created.

Cash basis reporting is concerned only with the business's checkbook. Cash inflows are treated as revenues of the period; cash outflows are treated as the period's expenses. These cash flows do not capture the earnings activities of the period. For instance, we may have sold merchandise to a customer at the end of the year. Thus the customer will not pay us until next year. On the cash basis, the sale will not be recorded until the collection is made in the new year even though the effort to generate the sale was made in the old year. Likewise, if the salesman will not be paid for that day's work until the next period, his salary is not yet expensed on the cash basis.

**Red Flags.** Accrual accounting provides a measure of a period's earnings activities. Comparing accrual income measures over time can give us a feel for what the company can do in the future. But it does not provide us with a measure of the company's liquidity—its ability to pay its debts as they come due.

Cash-flow accounting will not isolate the earnings activities of a period. However, it does provide us with a liquidity measure.

If we combine accrual-income measures with cash-flow measures, we have a base from which to estimate future operations, measure liquidity, and determine the timing between producing sales and collecting on sales. This combination takes place when we use both the income statement (see Key 35) as well as the statement of cash flows (see Key 47) in analyzing a company's financial health.

# 47

# STATEMENT OF CASH FLOWS

The statement of cash flows is like a bridge. Balance sheets tell us what a company's assets, liabilities, and owners' equity are at a point in time. But what about the changes that have occurred in the business between two balance sheet dates (from the end of one fiscal year to the end of another)? The statement of cash flows is this bridge. It describes all of the changes that have occurred in the balance sheet during the fiscal year in terms of their effect on cash. What changes in the assets, liabilities, and owners' equity provided cash? What changes in assets, liabilities, and owners' equity used cash? These questions are answered by a statement of cash flows.

Here is one format for presenting that statement.

XYZ, Ltd.
Statement of Cash Flows
For the Year Ended December 31, 2008

Cash Flows From Operating Activities:

| | | |
|---|---:|---:|
| Received from customers | $2,418,500 | |
| Paid suppliers and employees | (1,255,000) | |
| Dividends and interest received | 150,000 | |
| Interest paid | (260,500) | |
| Taxes paid | (320,000) | |
| Net cash provided by operating activities | | $733,000 |

Cash Flows From Investing Activities:

| | | |
|---|---:|---:|
| Received—sale of plant | 3,000,000 | |
| Received—sale of equipment | 550,000 | |
| Paid—new equipment purchases | (1,015,000) | |
| Paid—new plant | (4,950,000) | |
| Net cash used in investing activities | | (2,415,000) |

Cash Flows From Financing Activities:
    Received—sale of bonds          2,000,000
    Paid Dividends to shareholders      (90,000)

    Net cash provided by financing activities  1,910,000

Net Increase in Cash                          228,000
Cash at the Beginning of the Year              50,000

Cash at the End of the Year                 $278,000

"Net cash provided (used) by operating activities" is cash-basis net income (see Key 46). It includes all collections during the year from sales of merchandise or from providing services along with all dividends and interest received from investments, reduced by the payment of operating costs, including interest and taxes. A schedule reconciling accrual-based net income for the year to the cash collected from operating activities must accompany the statement of cash flows.

The ($2,415,000) subtotal relates to changes in the company's assets. Decreases in investments, property, plant and equipment, intangibles, or other assets indicate that sales have taken place, providing the company with cash. Increases in these same assets indicate that the company has purchased additional assets—a major use of cash.

The $1,910,000 subtotal relates to changes in the company's liabilities or owners' equity. Increasing debt or selling stock (ownership) will provide the company with cash. Decreasing liabilities (indicating payment of debt) and dividends to shareholders are major uses of cash.

Some transactions do not have a direct effect on cash. For example, a purchase of land on a long-term mortgage with no cash down payment does not affect the company's cash balance. However, for the statement of cash flows to be a complete bridge between two balance sheets, this transaction must be reported. Major investing and financing activities that do not directly affect cash will be summarized in a schedule that accompanies the statement of cash flows.

Analyzing cash flows is discussed in Key 55.

# 48

---

# CONSOLIDATED FINANCIAL STATEMENTS

The key to understanding consolidated financial statements is to realize that they are more or less the sum of the parts. They are the combined financial statements of a parent company and its subsidiaries. A parent/subsidiary relationship is created when a company acquires more than 50% of the common stock of another company. Because common stock is the voting stock of a corporation, acquiring more than 50% entitles the acquiring company (parent) to majority representation on the board of directors of the acquired company (subsidiary) and, thus, to control the affairs of that company.

Accounting principles require that the assets, liabilities, revenues, and expenses of majority-owned subsidiaries be included in the financial statements of their parents. In preparing the combined (consolidated) financial statements, accountants eliminate any transactions between the parent and its subsidiaries. If these transactions were not eliminated, the assets, liabilities, revenue, and expense of the combined company would be overstated.

For example, if the parent Z has lent $5 million to its Subsidiary X, it will have a $5 million "Receivable from Subsidiary X" (an asset) recorded. Subsidiary X will have a $5 million "Payable to Parent Z" (a liability) recorded. But because parent and subsidiary are treated as one company in the consolidated financial statements, it makes no sense to report these items. A company cannot borrow from, or owe to, itself. When the consolidated balance sheet is prepared, the parent's $5 million receivable will be canceled against the subsidiary's $5 million payable. If this were not done, consolidated assets and liabilities would each be reported as $5 million more than they actually are.

In consolidating the financial statements of a parent and its subsidiaries that are not wholly owned (the parent does not own 100% of the voting stock), "minority interest" is created. "Minority interest" is the owners' equity held by the other shareholders of the subsidiary. If parent Z owns 60% of Subsidiary X, there is a 40% minority interest. Because accounting principles will allow all of the assets and liabilities of a subsidiary to be reported in the consolidated financial statements, the portion of those assets and liabilities that "belong" to the minority shareholders must be labeled "minority interest." "Minority interest" may be shown on the consolidated balance sheet either as a liability (the amount the parent "owes" the minority shareholders) or as a part of consolidated owners' equity.

Another account that frequently appears on the consolidated balance sheet is "Excess of Cost Over Net Assets Acquired." This is purchased goodwill (see Key 23), an intangible asset that will be amortized (expensed) over a period of time not to exceed 40 years (see Key 24). Additional information on the activities of the subsidiaries will be included in the notes to the financial statements dealing with "segments" (see Key 11).

A consolidated balance sheet showing minority interest between stockholders' equity and noncurrent liabilities follows.

# Consolidated Statement of Financial Position

December 31, 2009 and 2008

| millions of dollars | | 2009 | 2008 |
|---|---|---|---|
| *Assets* | | | |
| Current assets | Cash | $ 188 | $ 116 |
| | Marketable securities—at cost, which approximates market | 1,328 | 325 |
| | Accounts and notes receivable (less allowances of $82 on December 31, 2009, and $89 on December 31, 2008) | 2,751 | 2,554 |
| | Inventories | 899 | 865 |
| | Prepaid expenses and income taxes | 393 | 340 |
| | | 5,559 | 4,200 |
| Investments and other assets | Investments and related advances | 606 | 680 |
| | Long-term receivables and other assets | 533 | 657 |
| | | 1,139 | 1,137 |
| Properties | —at cost, less accumulated depreciation, depletion, and amortization of $16,789 on December 31, 2009, and $15,381 on December 31, 2008 | 18,129 | 18,169 |
| | | $24,827 | $ 23,706 |
| *Liabilities and Shareholders' Equity* | | | |
| Current liabilities | Current installments of long-term obligations | $ 222 | $ 236 |
| | Short-term obligations | 165 | 174 |
| | Accounts payable | 2,543 | 2,289 |
| | Accrued liabilities | 998 | 872 |
| | Taxes payable (including income taxes) | 970 | 1,019 |
| | | 4,898 | 4,590 |
| Long-term obligations | Debt | 2,773 | 2,993 |
| | Capitalized leases | 308 | 327 |
| | | 3,081 | 3,320 |

| | | | |
|---|---|---:|---:|
| Deferred credits and other noncurrent liabilities | Income taxes | 4,238 | 3,997 |
| | Other | 497 | 469 |
| | | 4,735 | 4,466 |
| Minority interest | | 6 | 6 |
| Shareholders' equity | Common stock (authorized 800,000,000 shares; issued and outstanding as of December 31, 2009—257,634,285 shares; December 31, 2008—255,700,810 shares) | 2,114 | 1,875 |
| | Earnings retained and invested in business | 10,044 | 9,610 |
| | Foreign currency translation adjustment | (51) | (161) |
| | Total shareholders' equity | 12,107 | 11,324 |
| | | $24,827 | $23,706 |

# 49

# QUARTERLY STATEMENTS

Both the New York Stock Exchange and the Securities and Exchange Commission (SEC) require that listed or registered companies provide their shareholders with quarterly financial statements. The content of the quarterly report filed with the SEC (the 10-Q) is discussed in Key 16.

Quarterly financial statements are prepared only for the first three quarters of a company's fiscal year. (Fourth-quarter statements will not be prepared because annual financial statements will be issued at that time.)

Quarterly financial statements look much the same as annual financial statements. However, there are some major differences. Accounting principles require that the same methods of recording revenue, expense, assets, and liabilities be used in the quarterly statements as will be used to prepare the annual statements, but in quarterly reports it will be necessary to estimate most key figures. For instance, because taking a physical inventory count is time consuming and costly, it will be done only annually.

In order to prepare the quarterly financial statements, ending inventory for the quarter will be estimated. The annual tax rate must also be estimated so that quarterly taxes can be recorded at the rate the company actually expects to pay.

Accounting principles also require that seasonality in the quarterly statements be pointed out. For instance, suppose that the second quarter's sales are normally greater than other quarters' sales. This should be pointed out in the second quarter's financial statements. This has the effect of reminding the reader that sales are not level throughout the year.

Quarterly financial statements are usually presented as unaudited information. The CPA merely reviews the statements, saying nothing more than "I do not know of any material changes that must be made to make the statements conform to Generally Accepted Accounting Principles" (see Key 13 for a discussion of GAAP). But, the accountant has not made tests of the underlying accounting records to see if they support the figures in the financial statements—that would be an audit.

See Key 15 for a discussion of the difference between an audit and a review.

# 50

# EARNINGS PER SHARE

The key to understanding earnings per share (eps) is to realize that it is a simple, almost intuitive accounting measure carried (of necessity) to its most complicated, confusing extreme. Still, earnings per share is important—it is often cited as the single most used financial ratio—and you can understand it if you ignore the complications and concentrate on the purpose of this ratio.

Earnings per share is simply the earnings of the company divided by the number of shares of stock outstanding. When you examine a company's earnings over a period of several years, a pattern of growth or contraction may become apparent. Reducing the company's total earnings to a measure of earnings per ownership share helps an investor determine how successful the company is in creating earnings for individual shareholders. If a company sells additional shares of stock, for instance, you would expect total earnings to increase as a result of the additional investment received from owners. The additional shareholder investment might be used to build a plant or expand operations in some other way.

An increase in total earnings achieved in this way can be misleading. Suppose a company with 100,000 shares of stock outstanding issued an additional 20,000 shares of stock and expanded production facilities with the cash received. Assume, as a result, that the company's earnings increased from $200,000 to $220,000 per year. If an investor looks only at total earnings, an increase of 10% may appear good. But if we look at the earnings per share for the two years, we see a decrease:

Before investment eps = $200,000/100,000 shares = $2.00 per share
After investment eps  = $220,000/120,000 shares = $1.83 per share

As companies increase and decrease the number of shares outstanding—by issuing or retiring shares of stock, by combining with other companies, or by fulfilling obligations to convert bonds or to meet employee stock options—the eps figure relates the company's reported earnings to the number of shares of stock outstanding. The most basic equation for earnings per share is:

$$eps = \frac{earnings}{number\ of\ shares}$$

But now for the complications: Suppose there are preferred stockholders as well as common stockholders. If that is the case, some of the company's earnings must be paid as dividends to preferred stockholders just as interest must be paid on debt. Dividend payments to preferred stockholders are a cost of capital (like interest) and must be subtracted from earnings to determine the earnings available to common stockholders. (Interest is already deducted as an operating expense in calculating earnings.) So, if we are interested in the earnings per share for common stockholders, we must modify the eps equation to read:

$$eps = \frac{earnings\ available\ to\ common\ stockholders}{number\ of\ shares}$$

Suppose further that the company issued or retired common stock during the year. A correct calculation now requires that a weighted average number of shares be used as the denominator. (This average weighs shares by the number of months they are outstanding during the year. This takes into account whether the shares were issued near the beginning or end of the year.)

151

$$eps = \frac{\text{earnings available to common stockholders}}{\text{weighted average number of shares}}$$

When a company has issued preferred stock or bonds that are convertible to shares of common stock, or when it has stock warrants or options outstanding that entitle the holders to purchase stock, the calculation of eps becomes even more complex. Some of these items are essentially shares of common stock in that it is obvious that at some point they will be exercised and increase the number of shares outstanding. By the same token, it may be obvious that other items will never be exercised and thus will not result in an increase in common stock outstanding. On some items, of course, even experts would disagree.

When the company issues convertibles, accountants calculate two measures of eps and publish both of them with the income statement in the annual report. The two measures of eps are called *basic* earnings per share (containing only a weighted average of common shares *actually outstanding* in the denominator) and *diluted* earnings per share (with all items that could reasonably be converted to common stock counted as common shares).

It must be noted that when accountants treat an item as if it were converted into common stock—thus increasing the number of shares outstanding—an adjustment must frequently also be made to the numerator. For example, if an issue of convertible bonds is treated as if the bonds were converted into common stock, the accountant must also correct earnings by adding back the interest expense that would not have been subtracted if the bonds had actually been converted. Similar corrections must also be made for dividends holders of convertible preferred shares.

An example of the income statement presentation of earnings per share is shown below.

|                          | 2009   | 2008   | 2007   |
| ------------------------ | -----: | -----: | -----: |
| Earnings per common share |        |        |        |
| Basic                    |        |        |        |
| Earnings from continuing operations | $ 1.15 | $ .72 | $ .53 |
| Loss from discontinued operations | — | — | (.23) |
| Extraordinary item       | —      | —      | .12    |
|                          | $ 1.15 | $ .72  | $ .42  |
| Diluted                  | $ 1.12 | —      | —      |
| Average number of common shares outstanding | | | |
| Basic                    | 20,293 | 16,225 | 16,201 |
| Diluted                  | 22,615 | —      | —      |

**Red Flags.** Accountants must often use reference materials to guide them in making these calculations. For the layman, trying to follow eps calculations can be quite confusing. Diluted eps is the most complex calculation, being an attempt to reflect the effect of every event that would (if it happened) result in a reduction of eps.

Many analysts place special emphasis on the trend of a company's eps from quarter to quarter or year to year. While this trend may well be more useful than the absolute value of the eps in any one period, a financial statement reader would be well advised to treat this measure as any other ratio and apply the analysis approach discussed in Key 59.

# 51

# RATIO ANALYSIS

Ratio analysis is the basic analytical technique used in the analysis of financial statements. The key to understanding ratio analysis is first to understand what ratio analysis is, then to see how financial analysts and other readers of financial statements can employ this useful tool to gain insight into the content of an annual report. It is also necessary to understand that financial analysis—using ratios or other tools—is hard work. There is a common misunderstanding that learning the tools of financial statement analysis will immediately give you "secret knowledge" or "special insight" into annual reports that ordinary folks do not have. This is not true. Ratio analysis is a valuable tool for use in understanding financial statements—that much is true. But ratio analysis is a tool like a shovel is a tool. Once you acquire the tool, it will require hard work and diligence to obtain results.

First, what is a ratio? That part is not difficult. A ratio is a measure of relative size that is calculated by dividing one number into another. A ratio can be expressed in a number of ways.

4 divided by 3
4/3
4:3
4 to 3
1.33

The expressions above all show the ratio of four to three, but they are also the ratio of any other pair of numbers where the first is 1-1/3 times the second. The expressions above also are the ratio of 400 to 300, or 4 million to 3 million, or 12,000 to 9000 or 992 to 744, and so on. A ratio describes the relative size of two numbers or quantities but does not tell you the absolute size of the quantities being described. Each of the pairs listed, expressed as a fraction, reduces to 4/3, or, divided, equals 1.33.

A ratio also gives information about the two quantities used to generate the ratio. Assume the ratio of weight (in pounds) to height (in feet) for Bill Jones is 45:1. Can you make judgments about Bill based only on this ratio? Would Bill be a good pick for a basketball team? Using the ratio, we know that if Bill weighs 225 pounds, he is 5 feet tall (225/5 reduces to 45/1, or the ratio expressed as 45: 1, above). At 6 feet tall, Bill would have to weigh 270 pounds ($6 \times 45 = 270$) to have a weight-to-height ratio of 45:1. So Bill is probably not a good pick for a basketball team. For a football lineman, however, Bill may be a great pick! You cannot tell for sure, because you do not know the absolute values for his weight or height, but you can begin to form judgments from the relative measure of weight to height. Bill is a better pick for a football lineman, for instance, than is Ted Jones, whose weight-to-height ratio is 35:2. At 6 feet tall, Ted would weigh only 105 pounds ($35 \times 6/2 = 105$).

The same basic idea holds true for using ratios to make assessments of financial statements. Assume a company has assets of $10 million and liabilities of $6 million. The ratio of assets to liabilities is 5:3 (10:6 reduces to 5:3). What judgments can you make from this ratio? Is the company solvent?

Yes, the company is solvent, for assets are greater than liabilities. (The ratio of assets to liabilities is greater than one.) But does the company have an ideal level of debt? Should the company have more debt? Or less debt? Without a standard of comparison, you cannot tell. Above, when you were told "basketball team" or "football lineman," you had a standard of reference to judge Bill, for you know the general build of these players. Or, when you were given Ted as a comparison to Bill, you could make judgments about Bill's relative desirability. The same is true of ratio analysis for companies. If you know the general ratio for assets to liabilities for the company's industry (a standard of reference) or for its major competitor (a comparison), you can make a judgment as to the desirability of an asset-to-liability ratio of 5:3.

A ratio for a company can be compared to each of the following: (1) the company's industry average or standard, (2) another company in the same industry, or (3) the same ratio for the company in prior years.

A comparison with ratios of prior years gives a different perspective than does a comparison with ratios for the company's industry or competitor. A comparison with prior years may disclose a pattern. Assume, for instance, that the ratio of assets to liabilities for a company has gone from 5:2 to 2:1 to 5:3 during the last three years. Debt has increased—from 40% to 50% to 60% of total assets. Depending on other factors, this may be a cause of great concern.

Finally, you should note that more than one ratio is needed to make an assessment of the financial statements in a company's annual report. Ratios are available that help in analyzing profitability, solvency, activity, and liquidity. These ratios are described and analyzed in the succeeding four sections. A company's solvency ratios may be ideal, but if ratios that help analyze profitability and activity are bad (profits are down and sales are stagnant), a financial analyst would be concerned. You can only learn to use ratios in financial statement analysis by diving in and doing a bit of hard work. That is the key to understanding ratio analysis!

# 52

# PROFITABILITY RATIOS

Profitability ratios are usually "return on" ratios, measuring some aspect of management's operating efficiency. The numerator (the figure above the line) of a profitability ratio is usually some measure of net income or profit, and the denominator (the figure below the line) some aspect of the company that is management's responsibility.

Profitability ratios relate profit to some particular aspect of management performance: (1) return on assets, (2) return on owners' investment (or equity), or (3) return on sales. Profitability ratios that are used to measure management's performance on these three areas follow.

To measure management's success in employing assets profitably:

$$\text{return on assets} = \frac{\text{net income}}{\text{total assets}}$$

To measure management's success in maximizing the return on owners' investment:

$$\text{return on equity} = \frac{\text{net income}}{\text{owners' equity}}$$

To evaluate the profit generated on sales:

$$\text{return on sales} = \frac{\text{net income}}{\text{sales}}$$

Frequently the return-on-sales ratio is combined with the asset-turnover ratio so that the components of the return-on-assets profitability ratio can be studied. (Asset turnover can be defined simply as the number of times an asset is replaced during the period being analyzed.) The combination of these equations is called the DuPont method of financial analysis:

return on sales × asset turnover = return on assets

$$\frac{\text{net income}}{\text{sales}} \times \frac{\text{sales}}{\text{assets}} = \frac{\text{net income}}{\text{assets}}$$

Depending on the firm and the industry, a company may choose to stress either the return (or margin) on sales or the turnover and still generate the same return on assets.

Imagine a giant new car dealership with high turnover and low prices, and a tiny dealership with low turnover and higher prices. Both might generate the same return on total assets.

|  | return on sales | | asset turnover | | return on assets |
|---|---|---|---|---|---|
| giant dealer: | .05 | × | 6 | = | .30 |
| tiny dealer: | .15 | × | 2 | = | .30 |

There is another class of profitability ratios which relates the earnings reported by the company to the price of its stock or the dividend pattern established by management.

$$\text{price earnings (PE) ratio} = \frac{\text{common stock market}}{\text{earnings per common share}}$$

$$\text{dividend-payout ratio} = \frac{\text{dividend per common share}}{\text{earnings per common share}}$$

Both of these ratios are important to analysts. The price earnings ratio helps an analyst decide whether the stock is overpriced or underpriced in the market for the income the company is reporting. The PE ratio is considered so important that it is listed in the stock tables published daily in *The Wall Street Journal* and general newspapers with large financial sections. The dividend-payout ratio helps an analyst determine what management is doing with the earnings produced by operations: paying out a high proportion in dividends to yield greater current income to shareholders; using the earnings to finance company growth, and holding out the possibility of greater future profits; or using a balanced approach. Both of these ratios are important in establishing the price of the company's stock in the market.

# 53

# ACTIVITY RATIOS

Activity ratios measure management's effectiveness in using assets. These ratios generally involve a measure of the relationship between some asset, such as accounts receivable, and some surrogate for management's ability to employ the investment in the asset effectively.

The key to understanding activity ratios is to note that the general form of these ratios is an asset divided into the best measure of that asset's activity. The general form is:

$$\text{Activity Ratio} = \frac{\text{Best Measure of Asset Activity}}{\text{Asset}}$$

For accounts receivable, the best measure of the asset activity is sales. The less money tied up in uncollected accounts for a given volume of sales, the more money management will have for other purposes. In a company with annual sales of $1 million and $500,000 in accounts receivable at the end of the year, for instance, management's performance would be improved if more sales' dollars could be collected and accounts receivable reduced to $100,000.

Activity ratios are usually referred to as *turnover ratios*. Accounts receivable of $100,000 is said to have turned over ten times in a company with annual sales of $1 million. For a company that does credit business, all sales go through accounts receivable, like water through a water wheel. For sales to pass through accounts receivable $100,000 at a time (the average balance), accounts receivable would "turn over" ten times. The activity ratio "accounts receivable turnover" is:

$$\text{AR turnover} = \frac{\text{Sale}}{\text{Average AR}}$$

In the example above, the ratio is calculated as $1 million divided by $100,000 equals 10 times. When the turnover of accounts receivable is known, the average collection period (average time funds are tied up in the asset) can be calculated. If accounts receivable turn over 10 times in a 360-day year (a banker's year), the average collection period is 360 divided by 10 equals 36 days.

$$\text{Average turnover period} = \frac{360}{\text{Asset turnover}}$$

This relationship can also be used to calculate the number of days funds are tied up in any other asset once the asset turnover is known. Other common activity or turnover ratios are listed below.

$$\text{inventory turnover} = \frac{\text{cost of goods sold}}{\text{average inventory}}$$

$$\text{fixed-assets turnover} = \frac{\text{sales}}{\text{average fixed assets}}$$

$$\text{total-asset turnover} = \frac{\text{sales}}{\text{average total assets}}$$

# 54

# LIQUIDITY RATIOS

There are only two liquidity ratios in common usage. Both of these ratios are designed to evaluate the company's ability to pay its short-term obligations.

The first liquidity ratio is the *current ratio*, which is simply the relationship between current assets and current liabilities.

$$\text{current ratio} = \frac{\text{current assets}}{\text{current liabilities}}$$

Current assets are short-term assets that either are cash or will become cash in one year. Examples are receivables that will be collected in 90 days or inventory on hand that will be sold in the next quarter.

Current liabilities are short-term debts that must be paid in one year or less. Any part of a long-term debt that comes due in the next 12 months is also a current liability. Thus, accounts payable and next year's installment on a 40-year mortgage are both considered current liabilities.

The second common liquidity ratio is called the *quick* or *acid test ratio*.

$$\text{quick ratio} = \frac{\text{current assets} - \text{inventory}}{\text{current liabilities}}$$

In the quick ratio, inventory is removed from current assets because inventory is usually not directly convertible to cash. Generally, inventory is sold to create an account receivable, and the receivable must then be collected before cash is available to pay short-term creditors.

The rule of thumb is 2:1 for the current ratio and 1:1 for the quick ratio. These rules of thumb are often cited but are, in fact, relatively useless. To have meaning, a ratio either must be compared to the ratios of other companies in the same industry, or must be viewed as part of a trend for a particular company.

An analyst must ask questions: Is the company's liquidity (current ratio) increasing or decreasing? If so, are the changes appropriate for the economic climate in the company's industry?

Sources of industry averages are cited in Key 59.

# 55

# CASH FLOW RATIOS AND QUALITY OF EARNINGS

Cash flow ratios are used to examine the adequacy of a company's cash flows and the quality of its earnings. The *overall cash flow ratio* measures the extent to which cash flow from operations is adequate for the company's investing and financing activities. The ratio is calculated by dividing cash flow from operations by the total cash used for financing and investing activities. All three of these amounts are shown in the company's statement of cash flows. A ratio greater than one indicates that the company's operations generate more cash than is consumed in its financing and investing activities. A ratio less than one means that cash flow from operations is not adequate to fund the company's financing and investing activities.

$$\frac{\text{Overall Cash}}{\text{Flow Ratio}} = \frac{\text{Cash Flow from Operations}}{\text{Financing}\ +\ \text{Investing}}{\text{Cash Outflows}\ \ \text{Cash Outflows}}$$

**The Quality of Earnings.** Investors' perception of the quality of a company's earnings is derived from the extent the company's reported net income is accompanied by an inflow of cash from operations. Analysts believe that earnings accompanied by cash flows are worth more than earnings that are not. The quality of a company's earnings helps determine the market value of its stock. Lower perceived earnings quality results in lower market value stock.

Low quality earnings result when earnings cannot be sustained or when accounting procedures increase earnings without a corresponding increase in cash flow. High quality earnings can be sustained and are accompanied by cash inflows.

Earnings are not accompanied by sustainable cash flows when managers attempt to increase earnings by changing the timing of revenues and expenses. Managers, for instance, might delay certain maintenance procedures costing $100,000 until next year to improve profits this year. This will improve current-year earnings by $100,000 but will reduce earnings next year by the same amount. Managers might increase sales this year by relaxing credit standards, creating sales that will become a bad debts expense next year.

Investors also view reported earnings as lower quality when a company chooses an accounting method because it maximizes reported earnings. Companies that use straight-line depreciation or FIFO inventory are seen by investors as having lower quality earnings than a company that uses an accelerated depreciation method or LIFO inventory.[1]

*Cash return on sales* is a cash-flow ratio similar to the return on sales profitability ratio (net income/sales). These ratios help compare the company's ability to generate profit on sales with its ability to generate cash flow from sales. The *cash-flow-to-net-income ratio* compares cash from operations with net income from operations. Both cash flow ratios are useful in analyzing the quality of a company's earnings.

$$\text{Cash Return on Sales} = \frac{\text{Cash Flow from Operations}}{\text{Sales}}$$

$$\text{Cash Flow to Net Income} = \frac{\text{Cash Flow from Operations}}{\text{Net Income}}$$

---

[1]See Ayres, "Perceptions of Earnings Quality: What Managers Need to Know," *Management Accounting*, March 1994, pp. 27–29.

# 56

# OVERALL (DEBT AND EQUITY) RATIOS

The overall (debt and equity) ratios are sometimes called solvency ratios. While liquidity ratios assist analysts in examining a company's ability to pay short-term debt, overall or solvency ratios indicate the relative size of the claims of long-term creditors, compared to the claims or property rights of owners.

The existence of too much long-term debt places restrictions on management and increases risk to stockholders. Long-term debt increases the fixed charges against income each period. The times interest earned (TIE) or the fixed charge coverage ratios, both of which are defined below, assist analysts in evaluating the burden on a company's finances of fixed interest and other periodic charges (lease payments, for example). These ratios are similar to the rules of thumb that limit a consumer's house payment, or house and car payments, to a certain percentage of the consumer's income. The proportion of a company's income that can safely be consumed by interest and other fixed charges, however, varies widely, depending on conditions within each company and within the industry in which the company operates.

Another effect of high levels of long-term debt is added risk to creditors. As long-term debt increases, creditors grow reluctant to continue to lend the company money. Eventually, funds will not be available or will be available only at very high interest rates.

The common ratios used to evaluate a company's solvency or overall debt and equity position are as follows:

$$\frac{\text{times interest earned}}{\text{(or interest coverage)}} = \frac{\text{earnings before interest and taxes}}{\text{interest expense}}$$

$$\frac{\text{fixed charge}}{\text{coverage}} = \frac{\text{earnings before interest and taxes}}{\text{interest expense + lease payments}}$$

$$\text{debt to total assets} = \frac{\text{debt}}{\text{total assets}}$$

$$\frac{\text{debt to}}{\text{total equity}} = \frac{\text{debt}}{\text{total liabilities + stockholders' equity}}$$

$$\frac{\text{debt to}}{\text{stockholders' equity}} = \frac{\text{debt}}{\text{stockholders' equity}}$$

**Red Flags.** As mentioned above, too much long-term debt can be bad. This fact may bias readers of annual reports against long-term debt. But companies do not borrow without the desires of stockholders in mind. Managers use long-term debt to increase returns to common stockholders through financial leverage, as explained in Key 57. Long-term debt is not of itself bad, any more than using a mortgage to purchase a home is bad. The danger in both instances is in the level of total indebtedness and the burden of the resulting fixed payments.

# 57

## OPERATING AND FINANCIAL LEVERAGE

Leverage seems more properly a subject for a book on physics. There, it would be explained that when a lever is properly placed across a fulcrum, downward pressure on the handle results in a greatly magnified upward force on the other end. Ten pounds of downward pressure may be sufficient to lift a 100-pound weight. A child may lift a boulder with a lever, which gives the child a mechanical advantage.

There are two kinds of leverage managers can use to increase the profitability of a business to its owners: operating leverage and financial leverage. Both are very similar in principle to a child lifting a rock with a lever.

**Operating Leverage.** A company uses operating leverage to its advantage by balancing the mix of fixed and variable costs in its operations. Assume a company manufactures a product that it sells for $10. The labor and raw material costs for each unit of product (both are variable costs) total $8. Using a lot of labor, the company can manufacture the product with fixed costs (largely related to machinery) of only $20,000 per year. This is a fixed cost, remaining stable regardless of the number of units produced. With this balance of fixed costs and variable costs, each unit of product contributes $2 to covering the fixed costs and to building profits.

| Selling price | $10 |
| Labor and raw material | 8 |
| Contribution per unit | $ 2 |

Assume now that the company's managers decide to automate several previously manual operations. This increases the annual fixed machinery cost to $50,000, but the cost of labor and raw materials per unit is decreased to $6. Now each unit contributes $4 to covering fixed charges and to profit.

| | |
|---|---|
| Selling price | $10 |
| Labor and raw material | 6 |
| Contribution per unit | $ 4 |

Leverage increases the impact of a change in sales volume on the company's profits. Consider the contribution to profits of a 1000-unit increase in sales.

| Manual Operation | | Automated Operation | |
|---|---|---|---|
| Selling price | $ 10 | Selling price | $ 10 |
| Labor and raw material | 8 | Labor and raw material | 6 |
| Contribution per unit | $ 2 | Contribution per unit | $ 4 |
| Increased units | × 1,000 | Increased units | × 1,000 |
| Contribution | $2000 | Contribution | $ 4000 |

Changing the variable labor cost of operations to a fixed machinery cost has increased the contribution of a 1000-unit sale from $2000 to $4000. The automation has "leveraged" the effect of a sales increase on company profit.

**Red Flags.** Operating leverage has a down side. For instance, assume that instead of a 1000-unit increase in sales, the company had a 1000-unit decrease in sales volume. The effect is still the same dollar amount, but now the $2000 and $4000 changes in contribution are decreases, not increases.

Thus, highly leveraged companies generally have greater fluctuations in profits than companies with low operating leverage. A low-leveraged, manual operation does not benefit as much from increases in sales, but neither does it suffer as much from declines. Profits, by and large, will remain fairly stable. An automated, highly leveraged company, in contrast, will benefit greatly from sales increases and will suffer greatly from sales decreases. The contribution lost or gained will be greater, and the pattern of profits less stable.

Another warning about highly leveraged firms: the break-even sales point for a highly leveraged company is higher than the break-even point for a company with less leverage. In the example above, for instance, the company increased the annual fixed charges it had to cover from $20,000 to $50,000 when it automated. Break-even points for both operating structures are shown below.

*Manual operation:*

$$\frac{\$20,000 \text{ fixed cost}}{\$2 \text{ per unit contribution}} = 10,000\text{-unit break-even point}$$

*Automated operation:*

$$\frac{\$50,000 \text{ fixed cost}}{\$4 \text{ per unit contribution}} = 12,500\text{-unit break-even point}$$

In summary, operating leverage can improve a company's profits for a given level of sales, but to receive this benefit the company must endure the risk associated with an unstable profit pattern and an increased break-even sales level.

**Financial Leverage.** A company uses financial leverage to increase the return to owners. The idea is very simple. Assume that investors are forming a company that requires an investment in assets of $100,000. The company is projected to yield earnings of $15,000 per year. If owners supply the entire $100,000, the return on owner's equity will be 15% (15,000/100,000).

Now assume instead that the owners wish to leverage their investment by borrowing half of the $100,000 required to start the business. Funds are available at 12% interest. If the owners follow this route, investing $50,000 and borrowing $50,000 at 12% interest, there will be an annual interest charge of $6000 on the borrowed funds ($50,000 × .12), and earnings will be reduced to $9000. But the owners' investment has been reduced from $100,000 to $50,000, and the return on owner's equity has been increased to 18% (9000/50,000).

**Red Flags.** All companies use financial leverage to some extent. There is a great body of scholarly thought on just how great a proportion of a company's funding should come from debt and how much from owners. Too much debt increases business risk, and increased risk results in a company's having to pay higher interest rates on borrowed funds.

When interest rates are high, or return on assets is low, financial leverage may work against owners. Assume, for instance, in the illustration above, that the owners had to pay 20% interest on their borrowed $50,000. If the business does as expected and earns $15,000 before interest, the profit after an interest expense of $10,000 (50,000 × .20) will be only $5000 and the return on owners' equity will be reduced to 10% (5000/50,000).

Alternately, assume that the owners borrowed funds, as planned, at 12%, but that conditions changed and the company earned only $10,000 before the interest charges. After paying the $6000 interest on the debt, profits would be only $4000 and the return on owners' equity would be only 8% (4000/50,000). If owners had not borrowed at all, the return on owners' equity would have been 10% (10,000/100,000).

Both operational and financial leverage can be used to benefit stockholders. But both can be dangerous if business conditions change drastically. Both forms of leverage maximize the benefit obtained from growth, but both may also maximize the damage that occurs when business slows.

The extent to which a company uses financial leverage can be determined by examining a company's debt structure and profit pattern. Since companies list their costs by function and not by behavior, however, it is very difficult to measure operating leverage directly.

# 58

# COMMON SIZE STATEMENTS

Financial analysts sometimes use a variation of ratio analysis that looks at all the financial statement components. This method, called common size statements, presents every item in a statement as a percentage of the largest item in the statement. Although this procedure may sound confusing, common size statements are in fact quite useful and easy to understand.

Both the income statement and the balance sheet can be converted to common size statements. The largest item in the income statement is sales. Thus, when the income statement is converted to a common size statement, all items in the income statement are expressed as percentages of sales. For instance, if cost of goods sold is 40% of sales, gross profit would then be 60% of sales. Illustrations of a simple income statement and balance sheet converted to common size statements are shown below.

## INCOME STATEMENT

|  | Dollar Amounts | Common Size Amounts |
|---|---|---|
| Sales | $200,000 | 100% |
| Cost of Goods Sold | 80,000 | 40% |
| Gross Profit | 120,000 | 60% |
| Selling Expense | 30,000 | 15% |
| Administrative Expense | 50,000 | 25% |
| Operating Profit | 40,000 | 20% |
| Income Taxes | 20,000 | 10% |
| Net Income | $ 20,000 | 10% |

# BALANCE SHEET

|  | Dollar Amounts | Common Size Amounts |
|---|---|---|
| Cash | $ 500,000 | 16.6% |
| Accounts Receivable | 500,000 | 16.7% |
| Total Current Assets | 1,000,000 | 33.3% |
| Long-Term Assets | 2,000,000 | 66.7% |
| Total Assets | 3,000,000 | 100.0% |
| Current Liabilities | 1,000,000 | 33.3% |
| Long-Term Liabilities | 1,500,000 | 50.0% |
| Owners' Equity | 500,000 | 16.6% |
| Total Equities | $ 3,000,000 | 100.0% |

Common size statements highlight the relationship of all the statement components. Common size statements are especially useful when two years of the company are compared side by side, or when two companies of different sizes are being compared.

When two years of the same company are being examined in common size form, changes in the relative size of the components will be apparent to the analyst— changes that might have been missed by someone else, who was examining only the absolute dollar amounts. For example, if sales have increased, an analyst might not notice that gross profit has decreased by several percentage points, or perhaps that selling costs have risen sharply as a percent of sales dollars. When the two years are converted to common size statements, both of those changes will be obvious.

Analyzing the financial statements of two companies that are of different size is more confusing than analyzing two years of the same company's statements. Large differences in the dollar amounts of the various expense items will tend to camouflage differences in the relationship of the income statement components. Similarly, large differences in the proportion of the sales dollars spent on administrative expenses or debt service may go unnoticed if the statements are not converted to a common size format.

The largest item in the balance sheet is total assets, or total liabilities plus stockholders' equity. Thus, when a balance sheet is converted to a common size format, all components are expressed as percentages of total assets. For instance, current assets may be 40% of total assets. Bonds payable may be 30% of total liabilities plus stockholders' equity. (Remember that total assets and total liabilities plus stockholders' equity are equal. Either may be used.)

**Red Flags.** A variation of common size statements that is seen frequently can be constructed using the financial statements of some prior year as the base, and expressing the components of all future years as percentages of each component in the base year. For instance, advertising in the base year may have been $10,000, then in the next three years, $11,000, $12,000, and $20,000, respectively. Expressed in common size as a percentage of the base-year amount of $10,000, advertising would then appear as:

|  | Year 4 | Year 3 | Year 2 | Year 1 |
|---|---|---|---|---|
| Dollar Amount | $20,000 | $12,000 | $11,000 | $10,000 |
| Common Size Amount | 200% | 120% | 110% | 100% |

The jump to 200% in year 4 appears significant, but the large percentage increase could be misleading. Advertising may be a $20,000 expense for a company with total expenses of $800,000. In such case, the small dollar amount involved—while a large percentage increase—may be immaterial. Investigation would be a waste of time.

# 59

# FINANCIAL STATEMENT COMPARABILITY

Financial statement analysis is primarily a matter of making comparisons. A current ratio of 4:1 has no meaning by itself. It tells us only that current assets are four times current liabilities. But, if you find out that the company's current ratio for the past three years has been 2:1, 2:1, and 3:1, a pattern begins to emerge. (The current ratio is discussed in Key 54.)

For some reason, the current ratio is increasing. Is this good or bad? An excess of current assets is wasteful. Inventories may become obsolete. Receivable collections may be lax. On the other hand, too little invested in current assets relative to current liabilities is bad. Cash may not be available to pay creditors. Low inventory levels may cause stockouts. A comparison to prior years of the same company will help identify a trend but will not explain the cause or desirability of the pattern.

To determine the cause of an increase in the current ratio, we can look at the individual components of current assets and current liabilities. Most commonly, to determine the cause of an increase in the current ratio, we would look at the activity of accounts receivable and inventories. We might find that either accounts receivable turnover or inventory turnover had decreased because of larger balances in accounts receivable or more inventory stock on hand. A decrease in either of these ratios would help explain the increase in the current ratio. (Turnover ratios are discussed in Key 53.)

But even if we understand the cause of the current ratio increase to 4:1, we still do not know if 4:1 is good or bad. To assess the level of the current ratio, we must compare the company's ratio to ratios for other companies in the same industry. Composite ratios for different industries are published by Dun & Bradstreet, Standard & Poor's Corporation, Robert Morris Associates, and the Federal Trade Commission. An example of Dun & Bradstreet ratios is shown in the table below. These references can be found in most public or college libraries.

If we find that other companies in the same industry also have a composite current ratio of 4:1 (or close to it), we may feel that 4:1 is satisfactory. If we find that the industry current ratio is 2.5:1, we will be concerned by the increase from 2:1 to 4:1 over the last three years.

A company should always be analyzed by comparing its ratios (described in Keys 52–58) to the ratios of other companies in the same industry, or to the ratios of previous years in the same company. Comparisons to companies not in the same industry (comparing a bank to a paper mill) will generally have little meaning. You must remember that one ratio alone also generally has little meaning. You must calculate and compare ratios, measuring all facets of a company's activity and health (profitability, liquidity, activity, and solvency) if you are to make a clear analysis of the company's status.

# INDUSTRY NORMS & KEY BUSINESS RATIOS
## © DUN & BRADSTREET, INC.

| Industry | (times) Quick Ratio | (times) Current Ratio | (%) Total Liabilities to Net Worth |
|---|---|---|---|
| Agricultural Production | 0.9 | 1.8 | 63.9 |
| General Building Contractors | 1.3 | 1.7 | 99.7 |
| Newspapers | 1.6 | 2.2 | 57.0 |
| Petroleum Refining | 0.7 | 1.3 | 166.3 |
| Public Relations | 1.7 | 2.1 | 73.4 |
| Surveying Services | 2.1 | 2.5 | 48.7 |
| General Medical & Surgical Hospitals | 1.5 | 2.0 | 88.4 |
| Amusement Parks | 0.4 | 0.8 | 158.6 |
| Real Estate Agents & Managers | 1.3 | 2.0 | 55.7 |
| Jewelry Stores | 0.7 | 3.2 | 58.5 |
| Musical Instrument Stores | 0.4 | 2.3 | 97.5 |
| General Merchandise Stores | 0.9 | 3.9 | 47.4 |
| Natural Gas Distributors | 0.7 | 1.0 | 170.9 |
| Electric Service | 0.8 | 1.5 | 162.6 |
| Trucking & Warehousing | 1.2 | 1.5 | 97.7 |

# 60

# ANNUAL REPORTS OF FOREIGN COMPANIES

There is a move to harmonize accounting throughout the world, but a number of countries still produce financial statements that are difficult for investors in the United States to read and interpret. Typically, annual reports reflect the culture and economic climate of a company's home country.[1] Companies in North America, Great Britain, and the Netherlands use somewhat similar accounting methods, which focus financial statements on the needs of investors. This occurs because in these countries financial reporting is directed to the needs of capital providers. These countries have large markets for stocks and bonds, so published financial statements must be usable by different groups: individuals, institutions, banks, brokers, and others. In these countries, generally accepted accounting principals (GAAP) are developed in the private sector and often allow accountants to choose among equally acceptable methods of accounting for similar transactions.

In contrast, European companies often have close ties with only one source of capital, usually a large bank. Also, European GAAP historically has been established by law in each country and is often detailed and procedural, requiring strict compliance, with little room for judgment. European countries often use the same law to govern both taxation and financial reporting.

---

[1]This discussion of foreign culture and financial reporting is based on the discussion of "accounting clusters" by Mueller, Gernon, and Meek, *Accounting: An International Perspective*, pp. 8–13.

In South America, financial statements focus on accounting for the severe inflation common in that economy. South American financial reporting is structured to address the needs of government planners and frequently requires the same methods for both tax and financial reporting.

Financial reporting in Eastern Europe is continually changing as the former Communist countries find that, to obtain capital, they must evolve toward the more investor-oriented accounting models of Europe and North America. Under communism, there is no need to determine income and, with no need for calculating depreciation expense, fixed asset valuation is not important. Countries that retain state-operated industry still have no real financial reporting, but these operations are disappearing and financial reporting in Eastern Europe is rapidly adopting more informative accounting standards.

**How Foreign Companies Accommodate U.S. Readers.** Foreign companies that want to accommodate North American readers may use one of several methods.[2] The simplest method is to prepare convenience translations. There are three obstacles to reading the financial statements of a foreign company: language, monetary unit, and accounting principles. Because of this, convenience translations can take several forms. A company may translate the language, the monetary unit, the home country's GAAP, or any combination of these three. If a company translates only the language or the monetary unit, readers will still generally be aware that the statements are foreign; they may not be easily understood or comparable to the financial statements of U.S. companies.

If a company translates the language to English and the monetary unit to dollars, foreign statements may "look" like those of domestic companies, even though the earnings and other items are not comparable to the same items determined using U.S. GAAP. Foreign statements with

---

[2]Ibid, pp. 56–60.

179

the language and monetary unit translated—but not the GAAP—can be very dangerous unless you are an expert in the GAAP of the company's home country.

**International Accounting Standards.** The International Accounting Standards Board (IASB) represents more than 75 countries and is the most important international accounting standard setter. IASB accounting standards are establishing the tone and format for accounting and financial reporting in the international capital markets. Most IASB accounting methods closely resemble those in the United States. In most cases, a company in compliance with U.S. GAAP is also in compliance with IASB GAAP. In 2007 the SEC decided that foreign companies can use IASB GAAP in U.S. capital markets and are no longer required to present a reconciliation to U.S. GAAP.

**Red Flag.** Foreign stock offerings often attract attention. However, unless you read the company's home language and understand the company's home country GAAP, you will not be able to evaluate the company by its financial statements. Financial statement readers should be very cautious evaluating companies not traded on a U.S. stock exchange. If you want to invest in foreign companies, stick with those listed on a U.S. exchange or do it through a U.S. mutual fund that is either global or international. Global funds invest in the stocks of foreign and U.S. companies. International funds invest only in countries outside the United States, often in a particular geographical area.

Understanding financial statements is no easy task. It demands hard work and diligence. It requires an inquisitive mind and proper preparation. You have begun by reading this book. Good luck.

# QUESTIONS AND ANSWERS

**Q: How should I use this book?**

A: This book is put to best use when you read it with an annual report at your side. There are many examples and illustrations throughout the text, but you will gain a special perspective if you either (1) read this book and, as each annual report component is covered, look it up in an annual report, or (2) read through the annual report of a company in which you are interested and, topic by topic, refer to this book as a reference to increase your understanding.

**Q: What are the types of audit opinions a CPA may issue?**

A: A CPA may issue an unqualified opinion, a qualified opinion, or an adverse opinion, or a CPA may disclaim an opinion. When CPAs believe the financial statements are fair presentations of the company's financial position and earnings for the year, they issue an unqualified or clean opinion. A qualified opinion points out the particular area the CPA believes is not fair presentation. An adverse opinion states that the CPA does not believe the financial statements are fairly presented. A disclaimer of opinion means that the CPA is not expressing an opinion on the financial statements.

**Q: Does an unqualified audit report mean that the CPA recommends the company as a good investment?**

A: No. It only means that the CPA believes the financial statements are fair presentations of the company's financial position and earnings for the year. This belief is based on tests the CPA conducts on samples of the company's records.

**Q: Does an unqualified audit report mean that the company's financial statements are free of error?**

A: No. CPAs plan their audits to try to detect all material errors and irregularities. But their opinions are based on test samples of the company's records. Because they cannot test every record, it is possible that an error will go undetected.

**Q: Is a review the same as an audit?**

A: No. A review does not involve testing the accounting records from which the financial statements have been prepared. The CPA only questions management about the preparation of the financial statements and analyzes past and present financial statements to determine if unusual relationships exist. Where relationships appear normal the CPA does not investigate further. The review report will state that the CPA is not aware of any material changes needed to make the statements conform to generally accepted accounting principles. It will also state that the financial statements are unaudited.

**Q: Is Form 10-K the same as the annual report?**

A: No. Form 10-K must be filed with the SEC annually by publicly traded companies. While the 10-K contains the audited financial statements and much of the same information that companies include in their annual reports, it also contains additional, more detailed information.

**Q: Where can I find industry average ratios?**

A: Industry average ratios are published by Dun & Bradstreet, Standard & Poor's, Robert Morris Associates, and the Federal Trade Commission. Most public or college libraries will have one or more sources of industry ratios.

**Q: Why is pension and other retirement expense a significant part of many income statements?**

A: Reported pension expense is not the money paid to retirees during the year; more importantly, it represents the amount of money management should invest at the end of the year to cover future pension payments that are likely to be made to employees for this additional year's service. Management may choose to invest more or less than the current year's pension expense. Investing more than the current year's expense results in recording an asset, Prepaid Pension Cost. Investing less results in recording a liability, Unfunded Accrued Pension Cost. Actual payments to retirees are made from the pension fund investments.

**Q: Doesn't a balance sheet present the value of a business at a point in time?**

A: No. A balance sheet lists the resources and obligations of a business at a point in time. These resources and obligations are recorded at their original costs. No attempt is made to estimate the current values of the resources and obligations.

**Q: Why are there different methods to account for the same transaction? Is this to make it easy for companies to manipulate income?**

A: Different methods of accounting for the same transaction have developed over time as different accountants have looked at varying business practices and in good faith attempted to reflect the results of economic events in the accounts. Accountants may use several different methods of accounting for inventories and for productive assets depending on how the individual accountant believes the company has benefited from consuming the asset. Generally, straight-line depreciation (an equal amount each year) is used for assets from which the business benefits equally each year. An accelerated method of depreciation is used for assets that furnish most of their benefits during the early years of their lives. (A computer would probably be depreciated by an accelerated method.) The Financial Accounting Standards Board and others that set accounting standards attempt to resolve conflict when the choice between alternative accounting methods seems arbitrary.

**Q: Why are extraordinary items and discontinued operations shown separately in the income statement?**

A: Gains and losses that are not related to the main line of business or that occur infrequently are separately disclosed in order to allow comparisons of normal operating income between years. If we have an extraordinary gain this year and did not have one last year, it would only be appropriate to compare this year's income before extraordinary items to last year's net income.

**Q: What does it mean when a company labels its financial statements as "consolidated financial statements?"**

A: Consolidated financial statements are the combined statements of a parent company and its subsidiaries. Accounting principles require that the parent company combine the financial statements of its subsidiaries with its own when it owns more than 50% of the voting stock of the subsidiary.

# GLOSSARY

**Accrual** reporting concept that requires revenues to be reported in the fiscal period in which they are earned and expenses to be reported as they are incurred. Under the accrual concept, whether cash has been received or paid is irrelevant. *See also* Matching, Revenue Recognition.

**Allowance for Bad Debts** estimate of the dollar amount of accounts receivable that will not be collected, shown as a subtraction from total accounts receivable to calculate net (collectible) accounts receivable in the current assets section of the balance sheet.

**Amortization** assignment of the historical cost of an intangible asset to production periods as expense.

**Asset** anything of value that the business possesses and can use as it attempts to produce a profit.

**Auditor's Opinion** report issued by CPAs at the conclusion of an audit. The report will state that based on the auditor's examination, the financial statements are or are not fair presentations of the company's financial position and earnings for the fiscal year.

**Balance Sheet** financial statement that lists the assets, liabilities, and owner's equity of a business at a specific point in time.

**Bond** form of long-term debt, usually issued in $1000 increments, with interest paid semiannually and the principal repaid in 10 or more years.

**Book Value** value at which an item is carried in the books and displayed in the balance sheet. The book value of a depreciable asset is the asset cost minus accumulated depreciation.

**Capital Stock** *see* Common Stock.

**Certified Public Accountant (CPA)** accountant who has passed a standardized examination and has met the education, experience and other requirements of one of the states. A CPA is licensed to audit financial statements and express an opinion as to their fairness.

**Common Stock** ownership shares in a public corporation with the lowest preference as to assets on liquidation. Holders of common stock have the right to vote for the board of directors. In common usage, also called capital stock.

**Common Stock Equivalent** security convertible into common stock (as a convertible bond) or an option or warrant to purchase common stock.

**Comprehensive Income** the net change in owners' equity from transactions and events that did not involve the company's owners (i.e., omitting owner-transactions such as issuance and repurchase of stock and declaration and payment of dividends).

**Comprehensive Income Statement** contains a company's net income, plus any equity adjustments, such as any recognized holding gains or losses on debt, adjustments arising from "available for sale securities," foreign currency translation adjustments, or others from transactions and events that did not involve the company's owners.

**Conservatism** preference by accountants to place the lowest value on assets and income when faced with alternative valuations.

**Consolidated Financial Statement** combined balance sheets, income statements, and statements of cash flows of a parent company and its subsidiaries.

**Contingency** situation where a company stands to gain or lose because of a past transaction or event. The amount of gain or loss will be determined by a later transaction or event. Thus, a lawsuit creates a contingency; the amount of gain or loss is dependent on a later event, the judgment.

**Contributed Capital** personal investment made by the owners of a business. Contributed capital plus retained earnings equals owners' equity.

**Cost** *see* Historical Cost, Period Cost, Product Cost.

**CPA** *see* Certified Public Accountant.

**Cumulative Dividend** dividend agreement whereby a company must pay any dividends missed on preferred stock in past years before any dividend can be paid to common stockholders.

**Debenture** long-term debt instrument not secured by any lien on a specific property.

**Deferred Tax Liability** liability created when income reported on the income statement is not yet taxable but will become so in the future.

**Depletion** assignment of the historical cost of a natural resource to production periods as expense.

**Depreciation** assignment of the historical cost of a long-lived productive asset to production periods as expense.

**Derivative Financial Instruments (Derivatives)** financial assets or liabilities whose value is derived from the value of another financial asset, such as options or hedges.

**Donated Capital** the value of an asset donated to a company is recorded and the source of the asset is shown as an increase in owners' equity called Paid-in Capital from Donations.

**Extraordinary Item** after-tax gain or loss on an unusual transaction that is not expected to reoccur.

**Fair Value** *see* Market Value.

**Financial Accounting Standards Board (FASB)** independent board responsible for establishing accounting standards and concepts, founded in 1973 by the Financial Accounting Foundation as a successor to the Accounting Principles Board (APB).

**Fiscal Period** financial reporting period that may cover a year (fiscal year) or a quarter (fiscal quarter).

**Fixed Asset** *see* Property, Plant and Equipment.

**Generally Accepted Accounting Principles (GAAP)** accounting profession's collection of rules governing financial statement presentation and measurement.

**Historical Cost** total sum paid to purchase an asset and get it ready for use.

**Income from Continuing Operations** after-tax income of the portion of the business that is continuing.

**Intangible Asset** long-lived productive asset that does not have a physical existence. Intangibles include patents, copyrights, trademarks and tradenames, franchises, organization costs, and purchased goodwill.

**Interest Coverage** *see* Times Interest Earned.

**Internal Control** all the measures management puts in place to assure that information is gathered, recorded, and reported accurately and that assets are protected.

**Liability** any debt of the business; the amounts owed to nonowners.

**Market Value** an estimate of the amount that could be obtained upon sale of an asset at the balance sheet date. Such estimates can be based upon current selling prices of identical assets, current selling prices for similar assets, bid or ask prices for identical or similar assets, estimated cash to be received at the time of sale less additional cost to prepare for sale (net realizable value), or the present value of future net cash inflows from sale or use of the asset.

**Matching** principle that tells the accountant when to record a production cost as expense. Costs directly associated with producing a certain revenue will be expensed in the same period that the revenue is recorded. Costs that benefit more than one period are expensed over the periods benefited.

**Materiality** concept of relative importance. An item is material if it can influence a decision made by a user of the financial statements. When an item is material, it must be accounted for within the measurement and reporting principles—Generally Accepted Accounting Principles.

**Net Assets** assets minus liabilities. Net assets are equal to owner's equity.

**Net Income (Loss)** total of all reported revenues, gains, expenses, and losses for a fiscal period.

**Noncurrent Liability** any debt of the business that is not expected to be paid for at least one year from the date of the balance sheet.

**Obligation** *see* Liability.

**Operating Lease** leasing arrangement that does not transfer the risks of ownership to the lessee. The lessee will account for the lease payments as rental expense.

**Overhead** all indirect manufacturing costs (in contrast to the direct costs of labor and materials depreciation, property taxes, insurance, energy, supervisory labor, etc.).

**Owner's Equity** property rights of stockholders, calculated as assets minus liabilities; *see* Net Assets.

**Parent Company** company that owns more than 50% of the voting stock of another company.

**Period Cost** nonmanufacturing cost, such as administrative expenses, that is expensed as time passes rather than becoming part of the cost of a manufactured product and being expensed when the product is sold.

**Preemptive Right** right of common shareholders to maintain their proportionate ownership interest in a company by buying a like proportion of any new common stock issue.

**Preferred Stock** class of stock that is preferred over common stock as to dividend distribution or asset distribution in liquidation. Preferred shareholders generally do not have the right to vote on the board of directors.

**Premium on Bond Payable** difference between the face amount of a bond and the issue price when a bond is issued for more than face.

**Prepaid Pension Cost** asset created when a company invests more in its pension plan than the current year's pension expense.

**Price Earnings Ratio** market price of common stock divided by earnings per common share. This profitability ratio relates the market value of a company's common shares to the earnings per share of common stock.

**Product Cost** manufacturing costs assigned to products produced and held as an asset until the product is sold. Product costs are expensed when products are sold. *See* Period costs.

**Property, Plant and Equipment** long-lived productive assets, such as land, buildings, machinery, and furniture and fixtures.

**Receivable** any claim a company has against others that are expected to be settled in cash. Receivables are either trade (customers' accounts and notes receivable) or non-trade (as tax refunds, employee advances, or dividends receivable).

**Resource** *see* Asset.

**Results of Discontinued Operations** after-tax gain or loss on a segment of the business that management intends to sell.

**Retained Earnings** dollar amount of assets furnished by earnings of the company that were not distributed as dividends.

**Revenue Recognition** revenue is reported in the fiscal period in which the sale is made (or the service is provided) regardless of whether cash is collected from the customer or the customer still owes for the merchandise (service).

**Sarbanes-Oxley (SOX or Sarbox)** legislation that prohibits questionable activities and requires additional reports on internal controls over financial reporting.

**Securities and Exchange Commission (SEC)** federal agency created to administer the Securities Acts of 1933 and 1934. Although most accounting standards and concepts originated with the FASB or the APB, the SEC has final authority as to the accounting and reporting principles used in published annual reports.

**Serial Bonds**  bonds that mature (come due) in increments, as an issue of bonds that is structured so that 20% of the bonds mature each year after the fifth year.

**Statement of Cash Flows**  statement that reports all the changes that have occurred in the balance sheet during the fiscal period, either providing or using cash.

**Statement of Financial Position**  *see* Balance Sheet.

**Straight-line Depreciation**  method of depreciation that assumes equal benefit is derived from using a productive asset each year of its useful life. Depreciation expense will be the same each year under the straight-line method.

**Subsidiary Company**  company in which more than 50% of the voting stock is owned by another company.

**Times Interest Earned**  ratio of earnings before interest and taxes to interest expense. Sometimes called interest coverage. This ratio gives a measure of a company's ability to continue to service its debt if earnings decrease.

**Unearned Revenues**  current liability created by collecting from customers before they receive the merchandise or services for which they are paying.

**Unit of Measure**  currency being used in the financial statements. For U.S. companies the unit of measure would be the dollar, unadjusted for inflation or deflation.

# ACTUAL ANNUAL REPORT

**Tootsie Roll Industries, Inc.**

**Annual Report 2006**

CONSOLIDATED STATEMENT OF

# *Financial Position*

TOOTSIE ROLL INDUSTRIES, INC. AND SUBSIDIARIES

(in thousands)

## *Assets*

|  | December 31, | |
| --- | --- | --- |
|  | 2006 | 2005 |
| **CURRENT ASSETS:** | | |
| Cash and cash equivalents | $ 55,729 | $ 69,006 |
| Restricted cash | — | 22,330 |
| Investments | 23,531 | 54,892 |
| Accounts receivable trade, less allowances of $2,322 and $2,255 | 35,075 | 30,856 |
| Other receivables | 3,932 | 2,768 |
| Inventories: | | |
| Finished goods and work-in-process | 42,146 | 34,311 |
| Raw materials and supplies | 21,811 | 20,721 |
| Prepaid expenses | 6,489 | 5,840 |
| Deferred income taxes | 2,204 | 5,872 |
| Total current assets | 190,917 | 246,596 |
| **PROPERTY, PLANT AND EQUIPMENT, at cost:** | | |
| Land | 19,402 | 14,857 |
| Buildings | 87,273 | 63,544 |
| Machinery and equipment | 259,049 | 250,841 |
|  | 365,724 | 329,242 |
| Less—Accumulated depreciation | 162,826 | 150,482 |
|  | 202,898 | 178,760 |
| **OTHER ASSETS:** | | |
| Goodwill | 74,194 | 74,194 |
| Trademarks | 189,024 | 189,024 |
| Investments | 51,581 | 44,851 |
| Split dollar officer life insurance | 73,357 | 69,772 |
| Investment in joint venture | 9,668 | 10,499 |
|  | 397,824 | 388,340 |
|  | $791,639 | $813,696 |

(The accompanying notes are an integral part of these statements.)

193

# Liabilities and Shareholders' Equity

|  | December 31, | |
|---|---|---|
|  | 2006 | 2005 |
| **CURRENT LIABILITIES:** | | |
| Bank loan | $ — | $ 32,001 |
| Accounts payable | 13,102 | 17,482 |
| Dividends payable | 4,300 | 4,263 |
| Accrued liabilities | 43,802 | 44,969 |
| Income taxes payable | 1,007 | 14,941 |
| Total current liabilities | 62,211 | 113,656 |
| **NONCURRENT LIABILITIES:** | | |
| Deferred income taxes | 40,864 | 32,088 |
| Postretirement health care and life insurance benefits | 12,582 | 10,783 |
| Industrial development bonds | 7,500 | 7,500 |
| Deferred compensation and other liabilities | 37,801 | 32,264 |
| Total noncurrent liabilities | 98,747 | 82,635 |
| **SHAREHOLDERS' EQUITY:** | | |
| Common stock, $.69-4/9 par value— | | |
| 120,000 shares authorized— | | |
| 35,364 and 35,255, respectively, issued | 24,558 | 24,483 |
| Class B common stock, $.69-4/9 par value— | | |
| 40,000 shares authorized— | | |
| 18,390 and 18,000, respectively, issued | 12,771 | 12,500 |
| Capital in excess of par value | 438,648 | 426,125 |
| Retained earnings, per accompanying statement | 169,233 | 164,236 |
| Accumulated other comprehensive loss | (12,537) | (7,947) |
| Treasury stock (at cost)— | | |
| 62 shares and 60 shares, respectively | (1,992) | (1,992) |
| | 630,681 | 617,405 |
| | $791,639 | $813,696 |

194

CONSOLIDATED STATEMENT OF

# Earnings, Comprehensive Earnings and Retained Earnings

TOOTSIE ROLL INDUSTRIES, INC. AND SUBSIDIARIES

(in thousands except per share data)

|  | For the year ended December 31, | | |
|---|---|---|---|
|  | 2006 | 2005 | 2004 |
| Net sales | $495,990 | $487,739 | $420,110 |
| Cost of goods sold | 310,507 | 299,156 | 244,501 |
| Gross margin | 185,483 | 188,583 | 175,609 |
| Selling, marketing and administrative expenses | 99,233 | 96,936 | 85,705 |
| Impairment charges | — | 4,743 | — |
| Gain on sale of real estate | — | (21,840) | — |
| Earnings from operations | 86,250 | 108,744 | 89,904 |
| Other income, net | 8,465 | 4,908 | 4,784 |
| Earnings before income taxes | 94,715 | 113,652 | 94,688 |
| Provision for income taxes | 28,796 | 36,425 | 30,514 |
| Net earnings | $ 65,919 | $ 77,227 | $ 64,174 |
| Net earnings | $ 65,919 | $ 77,227 | $ 64,174 |
| Other comprehensive earnings (loss) | (3,697) | 2,984 | 778 |
| Comprehensive earnings | $ 62,222 | $ 80,211 | $ 64,952 |
| Retained earnings at beginning of year | $164,236 | $149,055 | $156,786 |
| Net earnings | 65,919 | 77,227 | 64,174 |
| Cash dividends ($.32, $.29 and $.27 per share, respectively) | (17,170) | (15,406) | (14,547) |
| Stock dividends | (43,694) | (46,640) | (57,358) |
| Cumulative effect of SAB 108 | (58) | — | — |
| Retained earnings at end of year | $169,233 | $164,236 | $149,055 |
| Earnings per share | $ 1.22 | $ 1.40 | $ 1.16 |
| Average common and class B common shares outstanding | 54,195 | 55,127 | 55,506 |

(The accompanying notes are an integral part of these statements.)

195

CONSOLIDATED STATEMENT OF

# Cash Flows

TOOTSIE ROLL INDUSTRIES, INC. AND SUBSIDIARIES

(in thousands)

For the year ended December 31,

| | 2006 | 2005 | 2004 |
|---|---:|---:|---:|
| CASH FLOWS FROM OPERATING ACTIVITIES: | | | |
| Net earnings | $ 65,919 | $ 77,227 | $ 64,174 |
| Adjustments to reconcile net earnings to net cash provided by operating activities: | | | |
| Depreciation and amortization | 15,816 | 14,687 | 11,680 |
| Gain on sale of real estate | | (21,840) | |
| Impairment charges | | 4,743 | — |
| Excess of earnings from joint venture over dividends received | (921) | (267) | (232) |
| Amortization of marketable securities | 909 | 1,680 | 1,885 |
| Purchase of trading securities | (749) | (1,141) | (1,796) |
| Changes in operating assets and liabilities: | | | |
| Accounts receivable | (4,368) | (1,846) | 673 |
| Other receivables | (4,125) | 1,519 | 1,574 |
| Inventories | (8,451) | 3,947 | (4,567) |
| Prepaid expenses and other assets | (1,912) | (4,357) | (4,822) |
| Accounts payable and accrued liabilities | (3,688) | (1,868) | 2,478 |
| Income taxes payable and deferred | (3,984) | 8,423 | 2,712 |
| Postretirement health care and life insurance benefits | 971 | 708 | 773 |
| Deferred compensation and other liabilities | 382 | 1,251 | 1,516 |
| Other | (143) | (342) | 180 |
| Net cash provided by operating activities | 55,656 | 82,524 | 76,228 |
| CASH FLOWS FROM INVESTING ACTIVITIES: | | | |
| Acquisition of business, net of cash acquired | | | (218,229) |
| Working capital adjustment from acquisition | | 6,755 | — |
| Proceeds from sale of real estate and other assets | 1,343 | 22,559 | — |
| (Increase) decrease in restricted cash | 22,330 | (14,690) | (17,948) |
| Capital expenditures | (39,207) | | (22,049) |
| Purchase of held to maturity securities | | | 44,113 |
| Maturity of held to maturity securities | | (16,772) | 83,987 |
| Purchase of available for sale securities | (35,663) | 46,350 | 134,061 |
| Sale and maturity of available for sale securities | 62,223 | | |
| Net cash provided by (used in) investing activities | 11,026 | 21,872 | (164,039) |
| CASH FLOWS FROM FINANCING ACTIVITIES: | | | |
| Proceeds from bank loan | | 38,401 | 154,000 |
| Repayment of bank loan | (32,001) | (98,400) | (62,000) |
| Shares repurchased and retired | (30,694) | (17,248) | (16,407) |
| Dividends paid in cash | (17,264) | (15,132) | (14,877) |
| Net cash provided by (used in) financing activities | (79,959) | (92,379) | 60,716 |
| Increase (decrease) in cash and cash equivalents | (13,277) | 12,017 | (27,095) |
| Cash and cash equivalents at beginning of year | 69,006 | 56,989 | 84,084 |
| Cash and cash equivalents at end of year | $ 55,729 | $ 69,006 | $ 56,989 |
| Supplemental cash flow information: | | | |
| Income taxes paid | $ 29,780 | $ 26,947 | $ 28,966 |
| Interest paid | $ 733 | $ 2,537 | $ 879 |
| Stock dividend issued | $ 43,563 | $ 46,310 | $ 56,959 |

(The accompanying notes are an integral part of these statements.)

# Notes to Consolidated Financial Statements *($ in thousands except per share data)*

TOOTSIE ROLL INDUSTRIES, INC. AND SUBSIDIARIES

## NOTE 1—SIGNIFICANT ACCOUNTING POLICIES:

### Basis of consolidation:

The consolidated financial statements include the accounts of Tootsie Roll Industries, Inc. and its wholly-owned subsidiaries (the Company), which are primarily engaged in the manufacture and sale of candy products. All significant intercompany transactions have been eliminated.

The preparation of financial statements in conformity with generally accepted accounting principles in the United States of America requires management to make estimates and assumptions that affect the reported amounts of assets and liabilities and disclosure of contingent assets and liabilities at the date of the financial statements and the reported amounts of revenues and expenses during the reporting period. Actual results could differ from those estimates.

Certain reclassifications have been made to the prior year financial statements to conform to the current year presentation.

### Revenue recognition:

Products are sold to customers based on accepted purchase orders which include quantity, sales price and other relevant terms of sale. Revenue, net of applicable provisions for discounts, returns, allowances, and certain advertising and promotional costs, is recognized when products are delivered to customers and collectibility is reasonably assured. Shipping and handling costs of $40,353, $37,836 and $31,795 in 2006, 2005 and 2004, respectively, are included in selling, marketing and administrative expenses. Accounts receivable are unsecured. Revenues from a major customer aggregated approximately 23.7%, 24.0% and 20.8% of total net sales during the years ended December 31, 2006, 2005 and 2004, respectively.

### Cash and cash equivalents:

The Company considers temporary cash investments with an original maturity of three months or less to be cash equivalents.

Restricted cash represents the net proceeds received from the sale of surplus real estate in 2005 which was held by a third party intermediary and earmarked for reinvestment in like-kind real estate as provided for in U.S. Internal Revenue Code Section 1031. During 2006, the Company reinvested such restricted cash in like-kind real estate.

### Investments:

Investments consist of various marketable securities with maturities of generally up to four years. The Company classifies debt and equity securities as either available for sale or trading. Available for sale are carried at fair value. Unrealized gains and losses on these securities are excluded from earnings and are reported as a separate component of shareholders' equity, net of applicable taxes, until realized. Trading securities relate to deferred compensation arrangements and are carried at fair value. The Company invests in trading securities to hedge changes in its deferred compensation liabilities.

### Hedging activities:

From time to time, the Company enters into commodities futures contracts that are intended and effective as hedges of market price risks associated with the anticipated purchase of certain raw materials (primarily sugar). To qualify as a hedge, the Company evaluates a variety of characteristics of these transactions, including the probability that the anticipated transaction will occur. If the anticipated transaction were not to occur, the gain or loss would then be recognized in current earnings. The Company does not engage in trading or other speculative use of derivative instruments. The Company does assume the risk that counter parties may not be able to meet the terms of their contracts. The Company does not expect any losses as a result of counter party defaults.

The Company's commodities futures contracts are being accounted for as cash flow hedges and are recorded on the balance sheet at fair value. Changes therein are recorded in other comprehensive earnings and are reclassified to earnings in the periods in which earnings are affected by the hedged item. Substantially all amounts reported in accumulated other comprehensive earnings (loss) are expected to be reclassified to cost of goods sold.

### Inventories:

Inventories are stated at cost, not to exceed market. The cost of substantially all of the Company's inventories ($61,092 and $51,969 at December 31, 2006 and 2005, respectively) has been determined by the last-in, first-out (LIFO) method. The excess of current cost over LIFO cost of inventories approximates $7,360 and $4,908 at December 31, 2006 and 2005, respectively. The cost of certain foreign inventories ($2,865 and $3,663 at December 31, 2006 and 2005, respectively) has been determined by the first-in, first-out (FIFO) method. Rebates, discounts and other cash consideration received from a vendor related to inventory purchases is reflected as a reduction in the cost of the related inventory item, and is therefore reflected in cost of sales when the related inventory item is sold.

### Property, plant and equipment:

Depreciation is computed for financial reporting purposes by use of the straight-line method based on useful lives of 20 to 35 years for buildings and 5 to 20 years for machinery and equipment. Depreciation expense was $15,816, $14,687, and $11,680 in 2006, 2005 and 2004, respectively.

### Carrying value of long-lived assets:

The Company reviews long-lived assets to determine if there are events or circumstances indicating that the amount of the asset reflected in the Company's balance sheet may not be recoverable. When such indicators are present, the Company compares the carrying value of the long-lived asset, or asset group, to the future undiscounted cash flows of the underlying assets to determine if an impairment exists. If applicable, an impairment charge would be recorded to write down the carrying value to its fair value. The determination of fair value involves the use of estimates of future cash flows that involve considerable management judgment and are based upon assumptions about expected future operating performance. The actual cash flows could differ from management's estimates due to changes in business conditions, operating performance, and economic conditions. No impairment charges were recorded by the Company during 2006, 2005 or 2004.

### Postretirement health care and life insurance benefits:

The Company provides certain postretirement health care and life insurance benefits. The cost of these postretirement benefits is accrued during employees' working careers. The Company also provides split dollar life insurance benefits to certain executive officers. The Company records an asset equal to the cumulative insurance premiums that will be recovered upon the death of a covered employee(s) or earlier under the terms of the plan. Split dollar premiums paid were $3,023, $3,678, and $3,620 in 2006, 2005 and 2004, respectively.

### Goodwill and Intangible assets:

The Company accounts for intangible assets in accordance with SFAS No. 142, "Goodwill and Other Intangible Assets." In accordance with this statement, goodwill and intangible assets with indefinite lives are not amortized, but rather tested for impairment at least annually. All trademarks have been assessed by management to have indefinite lives because they are expected to generate cash flows indefinitely. The Company has completed its annual impairment testing of its goodwill and trademarks during the fourth quarter of each of the years presented, and recorded an impairment of $4,743 in the fourth quarter of 2005 relating to a minor trademark and related goodwill. No impairments were recorded in either 2006 or 2004.

### Income taxes:

Deferred income taxes are recorded and recognized for future tax effects of temporary differences between financial and income tax reporting. Federal income taxes are provided on the portion of income of foreign subsidiaries that is expected to be remitted to the U.S. and become taxable, but not on the portion that is considered to be permanently invested in the foreign subsidiary.

### Foreign currency translation:

The Company has determined the functional currency for each foreign subsidiary. The U.S. dollar is used as the functional currency where a substantial portion of the subsidiary's business is indexed to the U.S. dollar or where its manufactured products are principally sold in the U.S. All other foreign subsidiaries use the local currency as their functional currency. Where the U.S. dollar is used as the functional currency, foreign currency translation adjustments are recorded as a charge or credit to other income in the statement of earnings. Where the foreign currency is used as the functional currency, translation adjustments are recorded as a separate component of comprehensive earnings (loss).

## Joint venture:

The Company's 50% interest in two companies is accounted for using the equity method. The Company records an increase in its investment in the joint venture to the extent of its share of the joint venture's earnings, and reduces its investment to the extent of dividends received. During 2006, dividends of $1,946 were declared and paid by the joint venture but not received by the Company until after December 31, 2006; this amount is included in other receivables at December 31, 2006. Dividends of $651 were received in 2005, and no dividends were received in 2004.

## Comprehensive earnings:

Comprehensive earnings includes net earnings, foreign currency translation adjustments and unrealized gains/losses on commodity hedging contracts and available for sale securities.

## Earnings per share:

A dual presentation of basic and diluted earnings per share is not required due to the lack of potentially dilutive securities under the Company's simple capital structure. Therefore, all earnings per share amounts represent basic earnings per share.

The Class B Common Stock has essentially the same rights as Common Stock, except that each share of Class B Common Stock has ten votes per share (compared to one vote per share of Common Stock), is not traded on any exchange, is restricted as to transfer and is convertible on a share-for-share basis, at any time and at no cost to the holders, into shares of Common Stock which are traded on the New York Stock Exchange.

## Recent Accounting Pronouncements

In July 2006, the FASB issued FASB Interpretation No. 48 "Accounting for Uncertainty in Income Taxes—an interpretation of FASB Statement 109" (FIN 48). FIN 48 prescribes a comprehensive model for recognizing, measuring, presenting and disclosing in the financial statements tax positions taken on a tax return. FIN 48 is effective for fiscal years beginning after December 15, 2006.

In September 2006, the FASB issued SFAS No. 157, "Fair Value Measurements" (SFAS 157). SFAS 157 establishes a common definition for fair value to be applied to U.S. GAAP guidance requiring use of fair value, establishes a framework for measuring fair value, and expands disclosure about such fair value measurements. SFAS 157 is effective for fiscal years beginning after November 15, 2007.

The Company is currently assessing the impact of FIN 48 and SFAS 157 and has not yet made any determination as to the effects, if any, that they may have on the Company's financial position and results of operations.

## NOTE 2—ACCRUED LIABILITIES:

Accrued liabilities are comprised of the following:

| | December 31, | |
| --- | --- | --- |
| | 2006 | 2005 |
| Compensation | $12,923 | $15,756 |
| Other employee benefits | 5,631 | 5,213 |
| Taxes, other than income | 1,781 | 1,765 |
| Advertising and promotions | 17,854 | 14,701 |
| Other | 5,613 | 7,534 |
| | $43,802 | $44,969 |

## NOTE 3—BANK LOAN AND INDUSTRIAL DEVELOPMENT BONDS:

Bank loans at December 31, 2005 are demand notes collateralized by certain investments in marketable securities. Interest was LIBOR based and averaged 4.6%. All bank loans outstanding at December 31, 2005 were repaid in 2006.

Industrial development bonds are due in 2027. The average floating interest rate was 3.6% and 2.5% in 2006 and 2005, respectively.

## NOTE 4—INCOME TAXES:

The domestic and foreign components of pretax income are as follows:

| | 2006 | 2005 | 2004 |
| --- | --- | --- | --- |
| Domestic | $81,514 | $103,725 | $89,164 |
| Foreign | 13,201 | 9,927 | 5,524 |
| | $94,715 | $113,652 | $94,688 |

The provision for income taxes is comprised of the following:

| | 2006 | 2005 | 2004 |
| --- | --- | --- | --- |
| Current: | | | |
| Federal | $14,358 | $33,036 | $26,303 |
| Foreign | 944 | 1,151 | 731 |
| State | 1,050 | 1,990 | 1,070 |
| | 16,352 | 36,177 | 28,104 |
| Deferred: | | | |
| Federal | 10,962 | 1,038 | 2,907 |
| Foreign | 1,196 | (849) | (605) |
| State | 286 | 59 | 108 |
| | 12,444 | 248 | 2,410 |
| | $28,796 | $36,425 | $30,514 |

Significant components of the Company's net deferred tax liability at year end were as follows:

| | December 31, | |
| --- | --- | --- |
| | 2006 | 2005 |
| Deferred tax assets: | | |
| Deferred compensation | $10,644 | $10,759 |
| Post retirement benefits | 3,938 | 3,759 |
| Reserve for uncollectible accounts | 567 | 506 |
| Other accrued expenses | 3,008 | 2,822 |
| Foreign subsidiary tax loss carry forward | 5,172 | 5,796 |
| Foreign tax credit carry forward | 4,900 | 2,312 |
| Marked to market on investments | 573 | — |
| Inventory reserves | — | 701 |
| Other | 687 | 1,206 |
| | 29,489 | 27,861 |
| Valuation reserve | (4,329) | (1,464) |
| Total deferred tax assets | $25,160 | $26,397 |

| | December 31, | |
| --- | --- | --- |
| | 2006 | 2005 |
| Deferred tax liabilities: | | |
| Depreciation | $22,330 | $21,992 |
| Deductible goodwill and trademarks | 22,447 | 19,373 |
| Accrued export Company commissions | 3,974 | 3,353 |
| VEBA funding | 897 | 748 |
| Inventory reserves | 2,591 | 2,287 |
| Prepaid insurance | 627 | 587 |
| Marked to market on investments | — | 1,423 |
| Deferred gain on sale of real estate | 7,972 | — |
| Other | 2,982 | 2,850 |
| Total deferred tax liabilities | $63,820 | $52,613 |
| Net deferred tax liability | $38,660 | $26,216 |

At December 31, 2006, the tax benefit of foreign subsidiary tax loss carry forwards expiring by year are as follows: $1,175 in 2014, $3,331 in 2015 and $666 in 2026. A valuation allowance has been established for these tax loss carry forwards to reduce the future income tax benefits to amounts expected to be realized.

Also at December 31, 2004, the amounts of the foreign subsidiary tax credit carry forwards expiring by year are as follows: $271 in 2007; $231 in 2008, $168 in 2009, $321 in 2010, $341 in 2011, $325 in 2012, $286 in 2013, $55 in 2014, $1,561 in 2015 and $1,341 in 2016. A valuation allowance has been established for these carry forward credits to reduce the future income tax benefits to amounts expected to be realized.

The effective income tax rate differs from the statutory rate as follows:

|  | 2006 | 2005 | 2004 |
|---|---|---|---|
| U.S. statutory rate | 35.0% | 35.0% | 35.5% |
| State income taxes, net | 0.9 | 1.2 | 0.8 |
| Exempt municipal bond interest | (0.8) | (0.6) | (1.2) |
| Qualified domestic production activities deduction | (2.8) | (2.8) | (1.9) |
| Foreign tax rates | (0.8) | (0.9) | — |
| Repatriation of accumulated foreign earnings | — | 0.7 | — |
| Other, net | (0.8) | (0.3) | (0.5) |
| Effective income tax rate | 30.7% | 32.3% | 32.2% |

The Company has not provided for U.S. federal or foreign withholding taxes on $6,561 and $8,831 of foreign subsidiaries undistributed earnings as of December 31, 2006 and December 31, 2005, respectively, because such earnings are considered to be permanently reinvested. It is not practicable to determine the amount of income taxes that would be payable upon remittance of the undistributed earnings.

American Jobs Creation Act of 2004 created a temporary incentive for U.S. corporations to repatriate accumulated income earned abroad by providing an 85% dividends received deduction for certain dividends from controlled foreign corporations. In 2005, the Company repatriated accumulated income earned abroad by its controlled foreign corporations in the amount of $21,200 and incurred a U.S. tax expense of $600 net of foreign tax credits.

## NOTE 5—SHARE CAPITAL AND CAPITAL IN EXCESS OF PAR VALUE:

|  | Common Stock | | Class B Common Stock | | Treasury Stock | | Capital in excess of par value |
|---|---|---|---|---|---|---|---|
|  | Shares | Amount | Shares | Amount | Shares | Amount |  |
|  | (000's) | | (000's) | | (000's) | |  |
| Balance at January 1, 2004 | 34,082 | $23,668 | 17,145 | $11,906 | (56) | $(1,992) | $357,922 |
| Issuance of 3% stock dividend | 1,009 | 701 | 356 | 513 | (2) | — | 55,961 |
| Conversion of Class B common shares to common shares | 143 | 99 | (143) | (99) | — | — | — |
| Purchase and retirement of common shares | (474) | (329) | — | — | — | — | (16,078) |
| Balance at December 31, 2004 | 34,760 | 24,139 | 17,515 | 12,163 | (58) | (1,992) | 397,745 |
| Issuance of 3% stock dividend | 1,033 | 717 | 524 | 364 | (2) | — | 45,229 |
| Conversion of Class B common shares to common shares | 39 | 27 | (39) | (27) | — | — | — |
| Purchase and retirement of common shares | (577) | (400) | — | — | — | — | (16,849) |
| Balance at December 31, 2005 | 35,255 | 24,483 | 18,000 | 12,500 | (60) | (1,992) | 426,125 |
| Issuance of 3% stock dividend | 1,048 | 727 | 539 | 375 | (2) | — | 42,461 |
| Conversion of Class B common shares to common shares | 149 | 104 | (149) | (104) | — | — | — |
| Purchase and retirement of common shares | (1,088) | (756) | — | — | — | — | (29,938) |
| Balance at December 31, 2006 | 35,364 | $24,558 | 18,390 | $12,771 | (62) | $(1,992) | $438,648 |

Average shares outstanding and all per share amounts included in the financial statements and notes thereto have been adjusted retroactively to reflect annual three percent stock dividends.

While the Company does not have a formal or publicly announced stock repurchase program, the Company's board of directors periodically authorizes a dollar amount for share repurchases

Based upon this policy, shares were purchased and retired as follows:

| Year | Total Number Of Shares Purchased | Average Price Paid Per Share |
|---|---|---|
| 2006 | 1,088 | $28.17 |
| 2005 | 577 | $29.87 |
| 2004 | 474 | $34.56 |

## NOTE 6—OTHER INCOME, NET:

Other income (expense) is comprised of the following:

|  | 2006 | 2005 | 2004 |
|---|---|---|---|
| Interest and dividend income | $2,615 | $2,632 | $3,784 |
| Interest expense | (726) | (2,537) | (912) |
| Joint venture income | 921 | 918 | 232 |
| Foreign exchange gains | 453 | 852 | 453 |
| Royalty income | 1,879 | 1,381 | 698 |
| Capital gains (losses) | 678 | 166 | (163) |
| Rental income | 1,940 | 1,107 | 413 |
| Insurance recovery | 300 | 326 | — |
| Miscellaneous, net | 405 | 63 | 279 |
|  | $8,465 | $4,908 | $4,784 |

## NOTE 7—EMPLOYEE BENEFIT PLANS:

Pension plans:

The Company sponsors defined contribution pension plans covering certain nonunion employees with over one year of credited service. The Company's policy is to fund pension costs accrued based on compensation levels. Total pension expense for 2006, 2005 and 2004 was $3,362, $3,362 and $3,174, respectively. The Company also maintains certain profit sharing and retirement savings-investment plans. Company contributions in 2006, 2005 and 2004 to these plans were $916, $905 and $806, respectively.

The Company also contributes to a multi-employer defined benefit pension plan for its union employees in the U.S. Such contributions aggregated $1,084, $1,011 and $1,007 in 2006, 2005 and 2004, respectively. Although the Company has been advised that the plan is currently in an underfunded status, the relative position of each employer associated with the multi-employer plan with respect to the actuarial present value of benefits and net plan assets is not determinable by the Company.

Deferred compensation:

The Company sponsors three deferred compensation plans for selected executives and other employees: (i) the Excess Benefit Plan, which restores retirement benefits lost due to IRS limitations on contributions to tax-qualified plans, (ii) the Supplemental Savings Plan, which allows eligible employees to defer the receipt of eligible compensation until designated future dates and (iii) the Career Achievement Plan, which provides a deferred annual incentive award to selected executives. Participants in these plans earn a return on amounts due them based on several investment options, which mirror returns on underlying investments (primarily mutual funds). The Company hedges its obligations under the plans by investing in the actual underlying investments. These investments are classified as trading securities and are carried at fair value. At December 31, 2006 and 2005, these investments totaled $33,800 and $27,500, respectively. All gains and losses in these investments are equally offset by corresponding gains and losses in the Company's deferred compensation liabilities.

Postretirement health care and life insurance benefit plans:

The Company provides certain postretirement health care and life insurance benefits for corporate office and management employees. Employees become eligible for these benefits based upon their age and service and if they agree to contribute a portion of the cost. The Company has the right to modify or terminate these benefits. The Company does not fund postretirement health care and life insurance benefits in advance of payments for benefit claims.

The Company adopted SFAS No. 158, "Employers' Accounting for Defined Benefit Pension and Other Postretirement Plans" (SFAS 158) as of December 31, 2006. SFAS 158 requires that employers recognize on a prospective basis the funded status of their defined benefit pension and other postretirement plans on their consolidated balance sheet and recognize as a component of other comprehensive income, net of tax, the gains or losses and prior service costs or credits that arise during the period but are not recognized as components of net periodic benefit cost. The effect of the adoption of SFAS 158 on the Company's consolidated statement of financial position at December 31, 2006 was an increase of $1,325 in the non-current liability for postretirement health care and life insurance benefits and a $893 increase in accumulated other comprehensive loss (net of tax effect of $432).

Amounts recognized in accumulated other comprehensive loss (pre-tax) at December 31, 2006 are as follows:

| | |
|---|---:|
| Prior service credit | $(1,252) |
| Net actuarial loss | 2,577 |
| Net amount recognized in accumulated other comprehensive loss | $ 1,325 |

The estimated actuarial loss, prior service credit and transition obligation to be amortized from accumulated other comprehensive income into net periodic benefit cost during 2007 are $215, $(125) and $0, respectively.

The changes in the accumulated postretirement benefit obligation at December 31, 2006 and 2005 consist of the following:

| | December 31, | |
|---|---:|---:|
| | 2006 | 2005 |
| Benefit obligation, beginning of year | $ 9,924 | $ 9,193 |
| Service cost | 524 | 474 |
| Interest cost | 539 | 519 |
| Plan participant contributions | — | 52 |
| Actuarial (gain)/loss | 2,101 | (103) |
| Benefits paid | (506) | (211) |
| Benefit obligation, end of year | 12,582 | 9,924 |
| Prior service cost | — | 1,377 |
| Net actuarial loss | — | (518) |
| Net amount recognized at December 31 | $12,582 | $10,783 |

Net periodic postretirement benefit cost included the following components:

| | 2006 | 2005 | 2004 |
|---|---:|---:|---:|
| Service cost—benefits attributed to service during the period | $524 | $521 | |
| Interest cost on the accumulated postretirement benefit obligation | 539 | 519 | 514 |
| Net amortization | (84) | (74) | (43) |
| Net periodic postretirement benefit cost | $979 | $919 | $992 |

For measurement purposes, the 2006 annual rate of increase in the per capita cost of covered health care benefits was assumed to be 9.0% for pre-age 65 retirees, 10.5% for post-age 65 retirees and 12.0% for prescription drugs; these rates were assumed to decrease gradually to 5.0% for 2014 and remain at that level thereafter. The health care cost trend rate assumption has a significant effect on the amounts reported. The weighted-average discount rate used in determining the accumulated postretirement benefit obligation was 5.60% and 5.50% at December 31, 2006 and 2005, respectively.

Increasing or decreasing the health care trend rates by one percentage point in each year would have the following effect on:

| | 1% Increase | 1% Decrease |
|---|---:|---:|
| Postretirement benefit obligation | $1,802 | $(1,481) |
| Total of service and interest cost components | $ 196 | $ (155) |

The Company estimates future benefit payments will be $368, $429, $480, $546 and $575 in 2007 through 2011, respectively, and a total of $4,286 in 2012 through 2016. The future benefit payments are net of the annual Medicare Part D subsidy of approximately $1,003 beginning in 2007.

## NOTE 8—COMMITMENTS:

Rental expense aggregated $1,132, $1,090 and $1,012 in 2006, 2005 and 2004, respectively.

Future operating lease commitments are not significant.

## NOTE 9—SEGMENT AND GEOGRAPHIC INFORMATION:

The Company operates as a single reportable segment encompassing the manufacture and sale of confectionery products. Its principal manufacturing operations are located in the United States and Canada, and its principal market is the United States. The Company also manufactures and sells confectionery products in Mexico, and exports products to Canada as well as to over 30 countries worldwide.

The following geographic data include net sales summarized on the basis of the customer location and long-lived assets based on their physical location.

| | 2006 | 2005 | 2004 |
|---|---:|---:|---:|
| Net Sales: | | | |
| United States | $450,591 | $445,405 | $387,280 |
| Foreign | 45,399 | 42,334 | 32,830 |
| | $495,990 | $487,739 | $420,110 |
| Long-lived assets: | | | |
| United States | $282,490 | $246,721 | $293,618 |
| Foreign | 55,014 | 57,160 | 58,098 |
| | $337,504 | $303,881 | $351,716 |

## NOTE 10—DISCLOSURES ABOUT THE FAIR VALUE AND CARRYING AMOUNT OF FINANCIAL INSTRUMENTS:

The carrying amount approximates fair value of cash and cash equivalents because of the short maturity of those investments. The fair values of investments are estimated based on quoted market prices. The fair value of the Company's bank loan and industrial development bonds approximates their carrying value because they have a floating interest rate.

The carrying amount and estimated fair values of the Company's financial instruments are as follows:

| | 2006 | | 2005 | |
|---|---:|---:|---:|---:|
| | Carrying Amount | Fair Value | Carrying Amount | Fair Value |
| Cash and cash equivalents | $55,729 | $55,729 | $69,006 | $69,006 |
| Restricted cash | — | — | 22,330 | 22,330 |
| Investments available for sale | 44,351 | 44,351 | 72,270 | 72,270 |
| Investments in trading securities | 30,761 | 30,761 | 27,473 | 27,473 |
| Bank loan and industrial development bonds | 7,500 | 7,500 | 39,501 | 39,501 |

A summary of the aggregate fair value, gross unrealized gains, gross unrealized losses and amortized cost basis of the Company's investment portfolio by major security type is as follows:

| | December 31, 2006 | | | |
|---|---:|---:|---:|---:|
| | | | Unrealized | |
| | Amortized Cost | Fair Value | Gains | Losses |
| Available for Sale | | | | |
| Municipal bonds | $44,532 | $44,293 | $ — | $(239) |
| Mutual funds | 57 | 58 | 1 | — |
| | $44,589 | $44,351 | $ 1 | $(239) |

| | December 31, 2005 | | | |
|---|---:|---:|---:|---:|
| | | | Unrealized | |
| | Amortized Cost | Fair Value | Gains | Losses |
| Available for Sale | | | | |
| Municipal bonds | $69,560 | $68,723 | $ — | $(837) |
| Mutual funds | 2,527 | 3,547 | 1,020 | — |
| | $72,087 | $72,270 | $1,020 | $(837) |

There were no securities with maturities greater than four years. The sale of available for sale securities in 2006 resulted in realized gains of $684. Gross realized gains and losses on the sale of available for sale securities in 2005 were not significant.

## NOTE 11—COMPREHENSIVE INCOME:

The following table sets forth information with respect to accumulated other comprehensive income (loss).

| | Foreign Currency Translation Adjustment | Unrealized Gain/(Loss) on | | Postretirement and Pension Benefits | Accumulated Other Comprehensive Earnings (Loss) |
| --- | --- | --- | --- | --- | --- |
| | | Investments | Derivatives | | |
| Balance at January 1, 2004 | $(12,157) | $480 | $(32) | $ — | $(11,709) |
| Unrealized gains (losses) | 193 | (595) | 2,594 | — | 2,202 |
| (Gains) losses reclassified to net earnings | — | 155 | (1,237) | — | (1,082) |
| Tax effect | — | 159 | (501) | — | (342) |
| Net of tax amount | 193 | (271) | 856 | — | 778 |
| Balance at December 31, 2004 | (11,964) | 209 | 824 | — | (10,931) |
| Unrealized gains (losses) | 1,036 | (184) | 4,186 | — | 5,038 |
| (Gains) losses reclassified to net earnings | — | 36 | (946) | — | (910) |
| Tax effect | — | 55 | (1,199) | — | (1,144) |
| Net of tax amount | 1,036 | (93) | 2,041 | — | 2,984 |
| Balance at December 31, 2005 | (10,928) | 116 | 2,865 | — | (7,947) |
| Unrealized gains (losses) | (296) | 263 | 880 | — | 847 |
| (Gains) losses reclassified to net earnings | — | (684) | (6,856) | — | (6,540) |
| Tax effect | — | 156 | 1,840 | — | 1,996 |
| Net of tax amount | (296) | (265) | (3,136) | — | (3,697) |
| Adoption of SFAS 158 (Note 7) | — | — | — | (893) | (893) |
| Balance at December 31, 2006 | $(11,224) | $(149) | $(271) | $(893) | $(12,537) |

## NOTE 12—ACQUISITION:

On August 30, 2004, the Company purchased certain assets and assumed certain liabilities from Concord Confections, Inc. and its affiliates (collectively Concord) including its 50% equity interest in a Spanish joint venture. Cash consideration paid of $218,229 was funded by the liquidation of $64,229 of marketable securities and a bank term loan of $154,000. The results of Concord's operations have been included in the Company's condensed consolidated financial statements since August 30, 2004. Concord holds a strong market position in the bubble gum category and its products are sold primarily under the Dubble Bubble brand name and trademark.

The acquisition has been accounted for under SFAS 141, "Business Combinations," and accordingly the purchase method of accounting has been used. The allocation of purchase price is based on management's determination and professional valuations of the fair value of the assets acquired and liabilities to be assumed. The final adjusted purchase price was allocated as follows:

| | |
| --- | --- |
| Calculation of adjusted purchase price: | |
| Cash consideration paid for net assets acquired | $218,229 |
| Direct transactions fees and expenses | 1,000 |
| Less—Adjustment to purchase relating to minimum working capital required | (6,755) |
| Total purchase price | $212,474 |
| | |
| Allocation of purchase price | |
| Net working capital | $ 6,818 |
| Step up of inventories | 1,622 |
| Investment in joint venture | 10,000 |
| Property, plant and equipment | 43,572 |
| Indefinite lived trademarks | 116,530 |
| Goodwill—deductible for income tax | 36,468 |
| Total purchase price | $212,474 |

The following table includes the unaudited pro forma net sales, net earnings and net earnings per share for 2004 as if the Company had acquired Concord as of January 1, 2004. Pro forma adjustments are necessary to reflect costs and expenses of financing the purchase, including additional interest expense relating to bank borrowings and the decrease in investment income reflecting the sale of marketable securities, and changes in depreciation expense resulting from fair value adjustments to net tangible assets.

| 2004 Combined Pro forma | |
| --- | --- |
| Net sales | $479,278 |
| Net earnings | $ 64,873 |
| Earnings per share | $ 1.20 |

The pro forma results are not necessarily indicative of what actually would have occurred if the acquisition had been completed as of the beginning of the presented periods, nor are they necessarily indicative of future consolidated results.

The unaudited pro forma combined financial information presented does not reflect any cost savings or synergies that might be realized, including the anticipated elimination of substantially all of the Concord historical senior executive compensation and other management expenses which aggregated approximately $3,872 net of income taxes for the twelve months of 2004. The pro forma results also reflect $495 of historical foreign exchange gains net of tax for 2004.

## NOTE 13—GAIN ON SALE OF REAL ESTATE:

During 2005, the Company sold surplus real estate and realized a pre-tax gain of $21,840. As of December 31, 2005, the Company had recorded a current income tax expense and related current income tax payable of $7,972 relating to this gain. During 2006, the Company invested the net proceeds, $22,330 of restricted cash as of December 31, 2005, in new real estate investments in compliance with U.S. Internal Revenue Code (IRC) Section 1031. Upon reinvestment of these proceeds, the Company reclassified the related current income tax payable to deferred income tax liability, since the income tax on such gain was deferred.

## NOTE 14—SEC STAFF ACCOUNTING BULLETIN NO. 108

In September 2006, the SEC issued Staff Accounting Bulletin No. 108, "Considering the Effects of Prior Year Misstatements when Quantifying Misstatements in Current Year Financial Statements" (SAB 108). Traditionally, there have been two widely-recognized methods for quantifying the effects of financial statement misstatements: the "roll-over" method and the "iron curtain" method. Prior to its application of the guidance in SAB 108, the Company used the "roll-over" method of quantifying financial statement misstatements, which focuses on the impact of a misstatement on the income statement (and net earnings), including the reversing effects. If any of prior year misstatements were, as adjustments to the carrying values including the reversing effect. If any of prior year misstatements were, as adjustments to the carrying values of assets and liabilities as of January 1, 2006 with an offsetting adjustment recorded to the opening balance of retained earnings. The Company previously evaluated these items under the "roll-over" method and concluded they were quantitatively and qualitatively immaterial, individually and in the aggregate. The following table, and accompanying footnotes, summarizes the effects of applying the guidance in SAB 108:

| | Period in which the Misstatement Originated | | | Adjustment Recorded as of January 1, 2006 |
| --- | --- | --- | --- | --- |
| | Cumulative Prior to January 1, 2004 | Year Ended December 31, | | |
| | | 2004 | 2005 | |
| Current assets (1) | $3,252 | $ — | $ — | $ 3,252 |
| Noncurrent assets (2) | 2,154 | (464) | 1,446 | 3,136 |
| Current liabilities (3) | (1,628) | (242) | (2,329) | (1,867) |
| Noncurrent liabilities (4) | (2,286) | | | (4,609) |
| Impact on net income (5) | $1.53 | $(706) | $(883) | |
| Net decrease to retained earnings (6) | | | | $ (59) |

(1) Primarily includes adjustments to (a) inventory relating to the calculation of a valuation reserve of $333 and (b) accounts receivable relating to the classification of estimated collectible accounts on the balance sheet which were previously classified as an offset to an accrued liability of $2,635.

(2) Primarily includes adjustments to (a) property, plant and equipment relating to depreciation expense over several prior years of $1,500; the timing of the recognition of a loss associated with the abandonment and disposition of a minor asset of $640 below; the timing of the recognition of a minor asset at retirement and an obligation of $1,446 which is partially offset by the related liability discussed in Note 4 (c) below; and (b) other assets relating to the carrying value of cumulative split-dollar life insurance premiums paid by the Company of $587.

(3) Primarily includes adjustments to (a) accounts payable relating to certain estimated liabilities recorded during various acquisition purchase accounting transactions which were not subsequently adjusted for the lower actual amounts paid of $640; (b) accrued liabilities relating to the balance sheet of estimated collectible accounts of ($2,635) as described in Note 1(b) above; and (c) income taxes payable and deferred to reflect the income tax impact of recording the items described herein of ($981).

(4) Primarily includes adjustments to (a) employee benefit obligations relating to the unintentional misapplication of certain technical GAAP requirements surrounding the establishment of employee disability obligations of $1,575, each of which are substantially offsetting; (b) deferred income tax liabilities for computational differences relating to the calculation and reconciliation of deferred tax liabilities of ($2,059); and (c) other long term liabilities relating to the timing of the recognition of a minor asset retirement obligation of ($2,143).

(5) Represents the net after tax effect for the indicated periods resulting from the above-described items.

(6) Represents the net after tax impact on retained earnings as of January 1, 2006 to record the initial application of SAB 108.

UNAUDITED PRO FORMA COMBINED INCOME STATEMENT OF TOOTSIE ROLL AND CONCORD FOR THE TWELVE MONTHS ENDED DECEMBER 31, 2004

# Report of Independent Registered Public Accounting Firm

To the Board of Directors and Shareholders of Tootsie Roll Industries, Inc.:

We have completed integrated audits of Tootsie Roll Industries, Inc.'s consolidated financial statements and of its internal control over financial reporting as of December 31, 2006, in accordance with the standards of the Public Company Accounting Oversight Board (United States). Our opinions, based on our audits, are presented below.

## Consolidated financial statements

In our opinion, the accompanying consolidated balance sheets and the related consolidated statements of earnings, comprehensive earnings, retained earnings, and cash flows present fairly, in all material respects, the financial position of Tootsie Roll Industries, Inc. and its subsidiaries at December 31, 2006 and December 31, 2005, and the results of their operations and their cash flows for each of the three years in the period ended December 31, 2006 in conformity with accounting principles generally accepted in the United States of America. These financial statements are the responsibility of the Company's management. Our responsibility is to express an opinion on these financial statements based on our audits. We conducted our audits of these statements in accordance with the standards of the Public Company Accounting Oversight Board (United States). Those standards require that we plan and perform the audit to obtain reasonable assurance about whether the financial statements are free of material misstatement. An audit of financial statements includes examining, on a test basis, evidence supporting the amounts and disclosures in the financial statements, assessing the accounting principles used and significant estimates made by management, and evaluating the overall financial statement presentation. We believe that our audits provide a reasonable basis for our opinion.

## Internal control over financial reporting

Also, in our opinion, management's assessment, included in the accompanying Management's Report on Internal Control Over Financial Reporting, that the Company maintained effective internal control over financial reporting as of December 31, 2006 based on criteria established in *Internal Control—Integrated Framework* issued by the Committee of Sponsoring Organizations of the Treadway Commission (COSO), is fairly stated, in all material respects, based on those criteria. Furthermore, in our opinion, the Company maintained, in all material respects, effective internal control over financial reporting as of December 31, 2006, based on criteria established in *Internal Control—Integrated Framework* issued by the COSO. The Company's management is responsible for maintaining effective internal control over financial reporting and for its assessment of the effectiveness of internal control over financial reporting. Our responsibility is to express opinions on management's assessment and on the effectiveness of the Company's internal control over financial reporting based on our audit. We conducted our audit of internal control over financial reporting in accordance with the standards of the Public Company Accounting Oversight Board (United States). Those standards require that we plan and perform the audit to obtain reasonable assurance about whether effective internal control over financial reporting was maintained in all material respects. An audit of internal control over financial reporting includes obtaining an understanding of internal control over financial reporting, evaluating management's assessment, testing and evaluating the design and operating effectiveness of internal control, and performing such other procedures as we consider necessary in the circumstances. We believe that our audit provides a reasonable basis for our opinions.

A company's internal control over financial reporting is a process designed to provide reasonable assurance regarding the reliability of financial reporting and the preparation of financial statements for external purposes in accordance with generally accepted accounting principles. A company's internal control over financial reporting includes those policies and procedures that (i) pertain to the maintenance of records that, in reasonable detail, accurately and fairly reflect the transactions and dispositions of the assets of the company; (ii) provide reasonable assurance that transactions are recorded as necessary to permit preparation of financial statements in accordance with generally accepted accounting principles, and that receipts and expenditures of the company are being made only in accordance with authorizations of management and directors of the company; and (iii) provide reasonable assurance regarding prevention or timely detection of unauthorized acquisition, use, or disposition of the company's assets that could have a material effect on the financial statements.

Because of its inherent limitations, internal control over financial reporting may not prevent or detect misstatements. Also, projections of any evaluation of effectiveness to future periods are subject to the risk that controls may become inadequate because of changes in conditions, or that the degree of compliance with the policies or procedures may deteriorate.

Chicago, Illinois
February 28, 2007

202

# INDEX